FINANCING THE SOCIAL RENTED SECTOR IN WESTERN EUROPE

RENEWALS 458-4574
DATE DUE

HOUSING AND URBAN POLICY STUDIES 13

OTB Research Institute for Policy and Technology
Delft University of Technology
Thijsseweg 11, 2629 JA Delft, The Netherlands
Phone +31 15 278 30 05
Fax +31 15 278 44 22
E-mail mailbox@otb.tudelft.nl
http://www.otb.tudelft.nl

Ministry of Housing, Physical Planning and Environment
The Hague, The Netherlands

FINANCING THE SOCIAL RENTED SECTOR IN WESTERN EUROPE

Editor:
P.J. Boelhouwer

Contributors:
P.J. Boelhouwer
A. Golland
V. Gruis
M. Oxley
J. Smith

Delft University Press, 1997

The series Housing and Urban Policy Studies is published by:

Delft University Press
Mekelweg 4
2628 CD Delft
The Netherlands
Phone + 31 15 278 32 54

This project was commissioned by the Bank for Dutch municipalities (N.V. Bank Nederlandse Gemeenten)

Editors: Hugo Priemus, Johan Conijn, Jacques van der Jagt
Translation: Nancy Smyth van Weesep

CIP-GEGEVENS KONINKLIJKE BIBLIOTHEEK, DEN HAAG

Financing

Financing the social rented sector in Western Europe / P.J. Boelhouwer (ed.)
- Delft : Delft University Press. - Ill. - (Housing and urban policy studies, ISSN 0926-6240 ; 13)
ISBN 90-407-1433-9
NUGI 655
Trefw.: financing ; social rented sector ; Western Europe

Copyright 1997 by Onderzoeksinstituut OTB

No part of this book may be reproduced in any form by print, photoprint, microfilm or any other means, without written permission from the publisher, Delft University Press, Mekelweg 4, 2628 CD Delft, The Netherlands.

CONTENTS

PREFACE

1 INTRODUCTION 1
1.1 Financing in the social rented sector in Western Europe 1
1.2 The objectives and research questions 3
1.3 The research design 5
1.4 The structure of this report 6

2 THE NETHERLANDS 7
2.1 Introduction 7
2.2 The institutional arrangements 8
2.3 Supervision 10
2.4 The subsidies for the social rented sector 11
2.5 Financing in the social rented sector 14
2.6 Risk and guarantees in the social rented sector 17
2.7 Opportunities for outside lenders 19

3 BELGIUM 21
3.1 Introduction 21
3.2 The institutional structure 22
3.3 Supervision 23
3.4 Subsidies for the social rented sector 23
3.5 Financing in the social rented sector 27
3.6 Risk and guarantees in the social rented sector 30
3.7 Opportunities for outside lenders 31

4 ENGLAND 33
4.1 Introduction 33
4.2 The institutional structure 34
4.3 Supervision 35
4.4 Subsidies for the social rented sector 37
4.5 Financing housing associations 40
4.6 Risk and guarantees for housing associations 44
4.7 Opportunities for outside lenders 44

5	**DENMARK**	47
5.1	Introduction	47
5.2	The institutional structure	48
5.3	Supervision	49
5.4	Subsidies for the non-profit rented sector	50
5.5	Financing in the non-profit rented sector	51
5.6	Risk and guarantees	55
5.7	Opportunities for outside lenders	56
6	**GERMANY**	57
6.1	Introduction	57
6.2	The institutional structure	58
6.3	Supervision	60
6.4	Subsidies for the social rented sector	61
6.5	Financing in the social rented sector	64
6.6	Risk and guarantees in the social rented sector	66
6.7	Social housing in the new Bundesländer	67
6.8	Opportunities for outside lenders	68
7	**FRANCE**	71
7.1	Introduction	71
7.2	The institutional structure	72
7.3	Supervision	74
7.4	Subsidies for the social rented sector	74
7.5	Financing in the social rented sector	77
7.6	Risk and guarantees in the social rented sector	80
7.7	Opportunities for outside lenders	82
8	**SWEDEN**	83
8.1	Introduction	83
8.2	The institutional structure	84
8.3	Supervision	85
8.4	Subsidies for the non-profit rented sector	85
8.5	Financing in the non-profit rented sector	88
8.6	Risk and guarantees	91
8.7	Opportunities for outside lenders	91
9	**SUMMARY**	93
9.1	Introduction	93
9.2	The institutional structure	94
9.3	Financial support from the government	95
9.4	Supervision and audit in the non-profit sector	97

9.5	Financing in the non-profit rented sector: source of funding	98
9.6	The risk and guarantee structure	100
9.7	The volume of demand for financing	101
9.8	Interest rates and the providers of capital	102
9.9	Financing opportunities for foreign lenders	103
REFERENCES		107

PREFACE

This study of the financing of the social rented sector in Western Europe is part of a large research program entitled "A Comparative Study of Housing Systems in Europe". Earlier studies have reported on: General Policy Framework (Boelhouwer and Van der Heijden, 1992), Financial Instruments (Papa, 1992), An International Comparison of Housing Expenses (Menkveld, 1992, 1993), Home Ownership in the European Community: Fiscal and Other Financial Instruments (Haffner, 1992), and Housing Management in the Rented Sector (Van de Ven, 1995).

Each of these reports compiled by the OTB Research Institute for Policy Sciences and Technology covers the same countries, namely Belgium, Denmark, France, the Netherlands, England, the former West Germany, and Sweden. An attempt has been made to avoid unnecessary overlap. In many respects, the reports are complementary, and where this is deemed necessary, references to the other ones have been included.

During the work on this project, the researchers have benefitted from the guidance offered by Mr. J.C.A. Polman and Mr. R. van Woerden of the Bank for Dutch municipalities (N.V. Bank Nederlandse Gemeenten). We appreciate the helpful comments and support they offered during the entire period of cooperation on this project.
We also would like to express our gratitude to the civil servants, researchers and organizations in the different countries who returned our questionnaire.

The original text of this report was edited by Ms. Dr. E. Sjoer. Ms. Drs. N.J. Smyth van Weesep translated the text into English, and Ms. C.W. Groeneveld took care of the lay-out.

Peter Boelhouwer

1
INTRODUCTION

P.J. Boelhouwer
A. Golland

1.1 Financing in the social rented sector in Western Europe

A major transition of the housing systems has been initiated in Western Europe in recent years. This change is related to general trends of privatization, deregulation, and decentralization. These trends have also affected the function and the position of the social rented sector. In the first place, they make it necessary to reconsider the ownership of the dwellings. At issue is whether the dwellings must remain the property of the state or be transferred to private non-profit organizations, or even to the occupants by giving them the opportunity to buy their homes. Many of the social landlords are also being challenged to reconsider their objectives: should they limit themselves to accommodating the households at the bottom of society, or should they adapt to the general trend of privatization and target the middle or even higher income groups? If the latter strategy were to be selected, it would also be appropriate to undertake activities of a more commercial nature. This would free up financial resources that the organizations could then utilize to promote their social mission.

Finally, social landlords need to become more self-reliant. Government subsidies are being curtailed; to be able to attract investment capital from elsewhere, the social landlords need to show that they are financially sound organizations. They will need to adjust to the demands made by the capital market. But the capital market itself is changing because of European integration. One aspect is that capital can flow increasingly freely between de member states of the Union. At least in theory, there is a growing international dimension to housing finance. In reality, it has so far remained limited, at least in the opinion of most of the participants at a conference on European Housing Finance, which convened in Bristol in 1993 (Bartlett and Bramley, 1994). They concluded that the markets of the member states remain essentially national markets. The reason is that many profound barriers prevent the development of international competition.

Nevertheless, the financial markets of Europe are strongly converging under the influence of internationalization, deregulation, and privatization. European integration has only stimulated this development, not caused it. Increased competition and technological improvements have generated less expensive products. But the downside of this improvement in efficiency is the growth of financial risk. According to Ball (1994), this brings about cyclical instability in the financial (residential) markets. Borrowing trends also seem to become increasingly procyclical, accentuating the swings of the market.

Partly because of these trends, national housing markets show increasing instability. Periods of major price increases are followed by substantial price falls (e.g. in England, Finland, Sweden, and Denmark). Obviously, such developments first affect the homeowner market. But European integration is also significant for the social landlords, at least in the opinion of Thomas, the director of the research department of the bank of Dutch municipalities BNG. Apart from various problems of an organizational nature, the introduction of a European currency will require some reflection on the part of the housing associations. One reason is that credit ratings will become much more important for the interest rates to be paid in the context of the European Monetary Union, according to Thomas. The expectation is that the monetary union will have a negative impact on the interest rates and the rate of inflation, especially in Germany and the Netherlands; the interest rates may increase by as much as 10 to 20 percentage points. But much will depend on how well the economically weaker countries of the European Union can control inflation. Thomas expects that the monetary union will make capital more mobile, which improves the possibilities for financing. But at the same time, the lenders will scrutinize the financial position of the individual housing associations, as well as that of the entire sector, and will critically assess their prospects (Klieverik, 1996, pp. 8-10).

The new position in which the social rented sector in Western Europe finds itself has consequences for the way financial management is set up in general, as well as for the financing of anticipated projects. The role of the state in making loans available to social landlords has been eclipsed. They have to resort to the capital market, directly or through mediating organizations. In order to obtain the required financial means in the market, the social landlords are required to develop a financially responsible mode of management. Financial continuity, creditworthiness, subsidies, and guarantees serve as important conditions. Especially the credit rating of the associations is a prime concern. It can be enhanced in various ways. Separate loans could be guaranteed by a larger organization or by the public sector. These organizations could also guarantee the proper execution of the duties of the individual social housing association and they can make certain that it retains sufficient assets (high solvability). But lenders are also greatly interested in how the public sector controls the housing market, as well as in the creditworthiness of the individual social landlord. It makes a big difference for the assessment of risk whether new housing developments will be operated entirely on market conditions, or whether the public sector is committed to subsidize part of the margin, which is generally not cost effective. For the same reason, a stable development of rents and other housing expenses is important. Will there be subsidies to help tenants pay their rents in the long run? Is it likely that low-income groups will accumulate rent arrears? And is it likely that middle- and higher-income groups will flock to the homeowner sector? A stable social rented sector is crucial to lenders. And a condition for stability is that market fluctuations must be dampened by government regulation.

1.2 The objectives and research questions

The preceding section outlined the background of an investigation of financing in the social rented sector in Western Europe. The project will cover the following seven countries: the Netherlands, Belgium, England, Denmark, Germany, France, and Sweden. It forms part of the multi-year research program entitled "Comparative Study of Housing Systems in Europe", which was initiated by the OTB in 1990. The program has already generated reports on the General Policy Framework (Boelhouwer and Van der Heijden, 1992), Financial Instruments (Papa, 1992), An International Comparison of Housing Expenses (Menkveld, 1992, 1993), Home Ownership in the European Community (Haffner, 1992), and Housing Management in the Rented Sector (Van de Ven, 1995). This report is closely connected to the one mentioned as the last one on the list. That study formed the point of departure for the present analyses. These analyses shed light on the ways in which the social rented sector is financed in the seven selected countries. In addition, they are meant to illuminate the differences in the structure of the social rented sectors. The objective of the present study may be phrased as follows:

The objective of the investigation is to determine whether or not the social rented sector in each of the countries in question is a potential target for future loans originating with external lenders.

The rationale for the study and its objective can be elaborated into the following research questions:

a) *How is the institutional structure of the social rented sector designed in the seven countries under study?*

For each case, a brief overview will be provided of the categories of social landlords that are currently active and of the share they have of the existing stock as well as of new construction.

b) *In what way does the government provide financial support to the social rented sector in the form of subsidies that are tied to either the tenants or the dwellings and what fiscal advantages, if any, does the government offer?*

The involvement of public agencies in the social rented sector will be briefly described. That overview will deal with the various subsidies on new construction, as well as the ways in which individual tenants are supported by contributions towards their housing costs, including an indication of the magnitude of these programs. In addition, indications will be provided of the magnitude of the subsidized construction program and the amount of subsidy available for each dwelling.

c) *What form does the public control over management by social landlords take in the seven countries?*

This question deals with the legal form of the organizations active in social rented housing provision. The description will elucidate the structure of responsibilities as well as the way in which public oversight has been shaped.

d) *How is the financing of new construction and renovation activities undertaken by social landlords arranged in the seven countries?*

This part of the investigation serves to establish which actors are involved in the financing of new construction in the social rented sector as well as the standard conditions that govern such loans.

e) *What risks and guarantees pertain to the social rented sector in the seven countries?*

The focus of the description in these sections is on the structure of guarantees and securities in the social rented sector. Information will be collected on specific loans contracted for specified new construction projects. In addition, an assessment will be made of the financial position of the social landlords, individually as well as collectively.

f) *What conditions are set on giving loans to social landlords in the seven countries and what risks can be identified?*

This concerns the specific conditions imposed by lenders to offer loans to social landlords in each of the seven countries.

g) *What is the estimated volume of the annual financing need among social landlords for the production of new dwellings in the seven countries?*

This estimate will be derived from the total volume of new construction initiated by social landlords in combination with the share financed by loans.

h) *How do the interest rates for loans to social landlords compare among the seven countries?*

The intention is to provide an average per country as the answer to this question. If strong fluctuations within a country have occurred, this will be elucidated.

i) Which lenders to social landlords are active in the countries under study and what is their market share?

The answer to this question will include a brief description of each of the organizations involved in this type of financing.

j) Which countries in Western Europe are of interest to outside lenders?

This question serves to structure an evaluation of the answers to the previous questions focused on the possibilities for external lenders to make capital available for new construction activities by social landlords.

1.3 The research design

The research project was carried out by the OTB Research Institute for Policy Sciences and Technology of Delft University of Technology, in cooperation with the School of the Built Environment of the de Montfort University in Leicester (U.K.). This cooperation forms part of the Centre for Comparative Housing Research, which was officially initiated in Leicester in the spring of 1996. The chapters containing the analyses of England and Germany were contributed by staff of the de Montfort University, the remaining chapters by staff of OTB.

The following procedure was adopted to answer the questions listed above. The first step was a review of the literature. Its starting point was formed by two recent publications issued by OTB and de Montfort University: Comparative Study of Housing Systems in Europe: Housing Management in the Rented Sector (Van de Ven, 1995), and Housing Policy and Rented Housing in Europe (Oxley and Smith, 1996). The significant information derived from these studies was supplemented by the evaluation of recent policy documents, research reports, and statistical data concerning the financing of the social rented sector in Western Europe. Yet not all questions could be answered in full on this basis. Therefore, a questionnaire was designed and mailed to selected informants in the seven countries to be covered by this project. This survey covered various government agencies, umbrella organizations of social landlords, financial organizations, and scientific institutes. The replies from each of the countries were deemed sufficient. These replies were compared, analyzed, and incorporated in the chapters dealing with the individual countries. It must be emphasized that this part of the investigation constitutes an exploratory stage of the project. The issues are so complex and change so rapidly, that a more thorough comparison of its various aspects requires a proper investigation. It would have to be conducted locally through a series of visits.

1.4 The structure of this report

Chapters 2 through 8 consist of the vignettes of the countries covered by the investigations. It was decided to work from a standardized format, whereby each topic can be easily compared across countries by referring to the section in question. In each chapter, Section 2 covers the institutional arrangements of the housing market in which the structure of the social rented sector is accentuated. Section 3 in each vignette provides a brief review of the way in which the social landlords are being supervised in the country in question. The subsidies for the social rented sector are elaborated in each Section 4. A distinction is thereby made between construction subsidies and subsidies for the management of the stock, on the one hand, and the housing cost subsidies and the ways in which rents are determined, on the other. Each Section 5 can be seen as the core of our report. These sections focus on the financing of the social rented stock. Much of the data on which these sections are based are derived from the questionnaire. To supplement these descriptions, Section 6 deals extensively with risk and guarantees in the social rented sector. Finally, the concluding sections of each chapter present the evaluation of the possibilities for external lenders to move into these markets. These sections are based on the information in preceding sections, which lends them the character of brief summaries.

The report concludes with a review of all the answers to the questions posed above in Section 1.2.

2
THE NETHERLANDS

V. Gruis

2.1 Introduction

Non-profit rented housing is found in all Western European countries. Yet the Netherlands occupies a special position among them by the sheer size of its social rented sector. By the end of 1993, the sector accounted for 39.9 percent of the total Dutch housing stock. Home ownership amounted to 45.8 percent, and the private and commercial rented stock made up for the difference of 12.8 percent (compare Table 2.1). The Dutch social rented sector also occupies a special place among the Western European ones because the overwhelming share of this stock is owned by private organizations, mostly non-profit housing associations (Van de Ven, 1995, p. 12).

Since the publication of the most recent memorandum on housing policy (MVROM, 1989), developments in the Netherlands have been characterized by deregulation, decentralization, and the granting of autonomy to the housing associations. The new policy entails the transfer of authority, of responsibility, and of risk from the national government to municipalities and provinces. Moreover, the housing associations and (organizations of) tenants have become autonomous.

Several legal instruments were introduced to implement the new policy, such as the statute for the management of the social rented sector BBSH, the statute for subsidies on construction and management BWS, and the new Housing Act.

The BBSH was issued in 1993 to redefine the responsibilities of the housing associations and to arrange for a new form of oversight. The new statute has vastly increased the power of the associations to devise their own policies. The regulations that used to prescribe their behavior were replaced by the principle of accountability for the management decisions initiated by the associations themselves. This increased freedom allowed the associations to establish their own rent policy by introducing the gross-rent principle: the associations are allowed to vary the rate of rent increases among their properties as long as the average increase conforms to the prescribed legal limit.

The decentralization of powers was brought about by the adoption of the BWS in 1992. This statute granted municipalities the prerogative of policy-making. They received budget authority for the new construction program and for the renovation of

Table 2.1　The tenure structure of the Dutch housing stock as of January 1, 1994 (percentages)

Ownership	
Homeowner	45.8
Private individual	7.9
Private organization (other than housing association)	4.9
Housing association	36.8
Public agency	3.1
Unknown	1.4
Number (x 1000)	6,306.7

Source: WBO 1993/1994, elaborated by OTB.

the pre-1940 housing stock. If the municipalities within a region have entered into mutual cooperation agreements, such regional bodies could assume budget authority. This change corresponded to the intent of the new system to promote regional cooperation.

The Housing Act ushered in a new regime of housing allocation. This change also reflects the trend toward decentralization. In this respect too, municipalities are free to establish regional cooperation, and they may transfer responsibilities to housing associations (Van de Ven, 1995, p. 11).

2.2 The institutional arrangements

The management of the social rented stock in the Netherlands is largely the responsibility of housing associations. These are private non-profit organizations set up for the explicit purpose of residential construction and housing management. Their activities are restricted to the field of housing. The Housing Act empowers the Minister to certify the associations as Accredited Institutions, and thereby they are qualified to receive subsidies.

There are about 800 of such housing associations in the Netherlands today, and together they own about two million dwellings. Most associations restrict their activities to a single municipality, but some operate regionally or nationally. Since the mid-1990s, the number of associations with a regional scope has increased rapidly. Their legal form is that of an association or a foundation. The main difference between the two is that in an association, the tenants are members, which allows them to be represented on its board. But to be able to deal effectively with their increased responsibilities, many associations are being converted into foundations. In most cases this means that the former directors constitute the executive, while the former board is transformed into a supervisory council. Because a foundation does not have members, the former members of the association lose the influence they used to exercise in the annual meeting of the members. However, the BBSH stipulates that the housing associations must consult their tenants before making policy decisions, whatever their legal form. The role of the tenants can be formally recognized in a contract binding tenants and board (Van de Ven, 1995, p. 13).

Not only the associations but also municipalities may manage social rented housing (they own 3.1 percent of national housing stock (WBO, 1993/94)). Many municipal housing authorities have been filing for the legal status of Accredited Institution. Formally, they will then no longer differ from the housing associations (Van Omme, 1992).

There are multiple ties between the national government, municipalities, and housing associations. The three consult each other intensively concerning all aspects of residential construction and management. The housing associations have several organizations at the national level: there are two major umbrella organizations, the NWR (Nationale Woning Raad) and the NCIV (Nederlands Christelijk Instituut voor de Volkshuisvesting). Moreover, there is a mutual funding organization CFV (Centraal Fonds voor de Volkshuisvesting) and a mutual guarantee fund WSW (Waarborgfonds Sociale Woningbouw). The function of the former is to support financially weak associations and, if necessary, to aid them in financial restructuring. The latter aim is meant to provide loan guarantees to limit the risk

Figure 2.1 The structure of the non-profit sector in the Netherlands

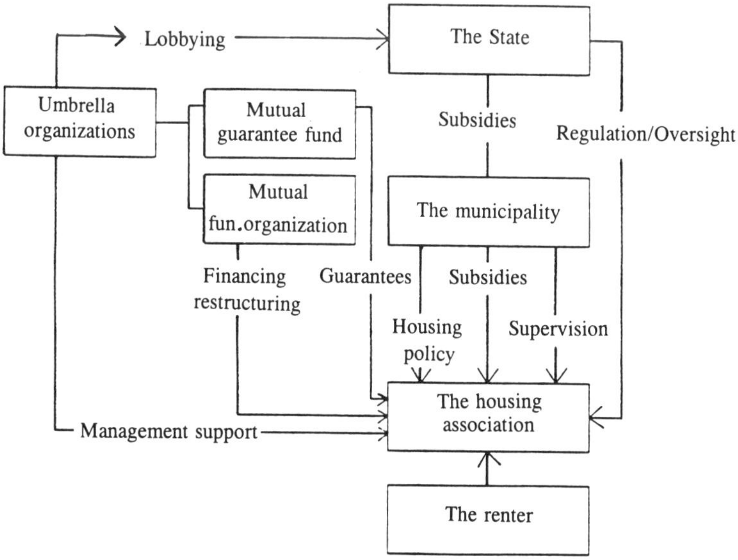

Source: Van der Schaar, 1991, p. 384.

of lenders; supposedly, this would lower the cost of borrowing and make more loans available. Many housing associations cooperate locally or regionally, and sometimes such cooperation is formalized in a federation. Figure 2.1 depicts the overall organizational structure of the social rented sector in the Netherlands (Van der Schaar, 1991, p. 384).

2.3 Supervision

Oversight of the housing associations is governed by the BBSH. This statute formulates four areas of responsibilities on which the performance of the associations is judged, namely:
- the accommodation of the target group;
- the quality of the housing stock;
- the involvement of the tenants in management and policy;
- the (financial) continuity of the operations.

In the near future, two areas of responsibility will be added (Van Noordenne, 1996; Kellersmann, 1996), namely:
- livability (of the residential environment);
- the social returns.

The associations have to submit an annual housing report and a financial report. In these documents, they must report on any progress that has been made in those areas.

Oversight of the associations is vested in the municipalities and is retrospective. The municipalities are not entitled to set prior performance standards. The statute assumes that the associations and the municipalities that have to judge their performance are in agreement on the desired performance (MVROM, 1992). If the municipality is dissatisfied, it may report its assessment to the Minister of Housing, Physical Planning and the Environment (VROM). Only the Minister has the power to impose sanctions on associations in the context of this oversight. The housing associations that also operate outside the municipal boundaries are supervised directly by the Minister (NWR, 1993).

There are exceptions to the principle of retrospective oversight: this applies to the so-called weighty decisions. In principle, this covers all decisions concerning the acquisition, mortgaging, sale, and demolition of dwellings, as well as the acquisition of a financial interest in or control over another legal entity (for instance, a form of cooperation with other associations). In such instances, the association must obtain prior permission from the municipality. But the BBSH allows associations and municipalities to agree on limiting the list of weighty decisions. Such an agreement might be based on considerations of limited financial risk or adverse effects for housing (NWR, 1993).

2.4 The subsidies for the social rented sector

Construction and management subsidies
Since 1992, the government has subsidized the construction of social rented dwellings with funds budgeted through the statute on subsidies for construction and management (BWS). This system of subsidies was streamlined in 1995. Until then, the subsidies were derived from four budgets (Van de Ven, 1995, p.19):
- a budget for the annual contributions for social rented dwellings, social home-owner dwellings, and for major renovations of dwellings built before 1940;
- a budget for supplements to compensate for adverse local circumstances;
- a budget for supplements to allow rent decreases;
- a budget for rented dwellings owned by private investors and for dwellings built with a one-time subsidy.

The BWS'95 introduced a comprehensive budget provided by the national government to municipal and regional housing funds (Heerma, 1993). The new approach marks the transition from generic policy to specific policy. Budgets and allocations are increasingly tailored to specific local conditions. Future budget managers (municipalities and regions) can then target the assets of the housing fund to the areas of greatest need. Moreover, their authority will be expanded.

The budget is fed by four subsidy flows:
- promotion of new construction;
- promotion of thorough improvements for (private) rented dwellings;
- supplements for locally different circumstances;
- supplements to improve access.

The total volume of the subsidy flows is determined at the national level on the basis of normative amounts.

The BWS'95 terminated the periodic subsidy on the operation of social rented housing. Annual contributions are no longer disbursed during the period of operation. They have been replaced by a single contribution granted when the dwelling becomes available for occupancy. For some 90 percent of the new social rented dwellings, the amount of NLG 5,000 is made available. Also approximately 45 percent of the somewhat more expensive new dwellings will qualify for this single financial incentive of NLG 5,000.

The supplements to improve access are meant to make social rented housing built in the new city extension areas (VINEX locations) accessible --also financially-- for large families and for the lowest income groups. This is intended to promote the differentiation of the stock. The supplements for locally different circumstances are partly motivated by the desire to promote the construction of more expensive dwellings within the existing urban areas, especially in urban renewal areas. Also this program is meant to increase the differentiation of the stock.

The BWS'95 also marks the transition to residential construction without subsidies. In the future, the various actors involved in housing will have to resolve their administrative and financial problems on their own (Van de Ven, 1995, p. 19).

Most of the subsidy commitments of the national government have already been canceled as the result of the recent so-called "grossing and balancing" operation. All construction subsidies that would have been payable to the accredited institutions after January 1, 1995 on the basis of regulations predating the 1992 BWS have been offset by the debts of these institutions to the state incurred for the construction of new dwellings (Van Middelaar, 1995).

As the operating subsidies are abolished, the associations themselves will have to deal with the investments in social rented dwellings that are not cost effective. One of the proposals being considered to this end is that of a revolving fund. The government considers the sector of social rented housing in its entirety as a revolving fund that should be able to function without government subsidies (Van Dieten, 1996). The idea of the revolving fund implies that current and future reserves generated in the social rented sector are put to use within that sector; this implies that the housing associations subsidize themselves. The revolving fund applies both to the sector as a whole and to the individual associations. Each one of them has to use the yields of their operations in the current stock to pay for (not cost-effective) new investments in the quality of the stock, new construction, and improvements in livability. For the sector as a whole, the yields of wealthy and poor associations can be balanced. For instance, rich associations could support their "poor relations" by lending them the needed funds at below-market interest rates. There may be a role for the CFV also. The annual contributions of the associations to this fund have created a situation in which the CFV manages a substantial part of the assets of the sector. These could be used to set up the revolving fund in the sector. This principle is already applied whenever the CFV provides financial support to an association in financial straits (compare Section 2.6). If the sector succeeds to operate as a revolving fund, it would create the unique situation of a social housing system that is not dependent on extensive public subsidies.

Rent subsidies and the determination of rent levels
Rent subsidies (IHS) were introduced in the Netherlands to ensure that the target group could afford to pay for social rented housing. Now, specific categories of tenants of social as well as private rented housing are entitled to these subsidies.

The avowed goal of the IHS program is to ensure the affordability of housing for specific income groups. The system became fully operational on July 1, 1975. The idea was that the amount of rent to be paid should not exceed a reasonable proportion of the household income. Ceilings were set on rent and income levels to qualify for the program. For each income category, a normative rent level was determined. More details of the program may be gleaned from Papa (1992, p. 19 *passim*).

To cap the program expenditure, the allocation of rented dwellings that would result in a subsidy claim of more than a given amount per month (NLG 300 in 1994) has been curtailed. But the rule does not apply to adapted or single-floor housing for the elderly or for handicapped persons (Van de Ven, 1995, p. 23).

The future of the IHS program is currently being reviewed. Housing Minister Tommel intends to change the program significantly by July 1, 1997. The changes would refocus the program on the lowest income groups. To this end, many responsibilities for the administration of the program would be transferred to local authorities. Contractual agreements are envisioned to restrict the allocation of dwellings to the target groups. New rent ceilings are to be determined. Dwellings with a rent above the norm can be allocated to households from the target group only in exceptional circumstances. According to the proposal, the determination of the ceilings will not only take account of income but also of the size of the household (Bouwmans, 1996).

The rent follows largely from governmental policy. The authorities regulate the rent levels and subsequent increases by law. These limitations are arranged by means of the gross-rent approach and the Dwelling Appraisal System (WWS). The housing associations determine the actual rent within this legal framework and the market conditions (Gruis, 1996).

The gross-rent approach has been specified in the Law on rents of living accommodation (HPW), the ministerial Decision on rents of living accommodation, and the BBSH. The gross-rent approach gives the associations the option to vary the rent increases of the individual dwellings they manage. Each year on July 1, when the rents are increased across the board, the associations may determine by what percentage the rent of each of their dwellings is to be increased (or decreased). Their leeway is curtailed by two givens. First, the rent cannot be increased by more than the maximum percentage determined by the Minister. Second, the total rent yield of the associations has to increase by a rate anywhere within the range set by the Minister (SEV, 1992). The associations are allowed to demand a larger increase in the case of a vacancy. But even then, the total rent increase realized by the association has to stay within the range set by law.

For each dwelling, the WWS sets a ceiling of the reasonable rent. This principle is also recognized in the HPW. The WWS applies to the social rented and to the market sector. The system quantifies various amenities of dwellings as scores on a rating scale. The maximum reasonable rent is derived from the number of points a dwelling is assigned. The contract rent may not be greater than this amount.

In addition to the constraints of the law and of the market, the rent is further determined by the degree to which the investments can be recouped. The important point for the associations is that the earnings should allow them to meet their obligations to repay the loans and whether or not there is a need to pay for the part they can not recoup through rents from their assets. The degree to which each association can afford to pay for investments that are not cost effective depends on their overall financial situation, on the requirements concerning assets made by lenders, and the degree to which the sector as a whole will be able to operate as a revolving fund.

2.5 Financing in the social rented sector

The construction of social rented dwellings in the Netherlands is generally financed with borrowed money. Only a small part of the financing is drawn from the principal's own assets. With the introduction of BWS'95, construction subsidies were curtailed. It is estimated that approximately 85 percent of the cost of new dwellings is financed by external funds, some 9 percent by own assets, and on average 8 percent by BWS subsidies (OTB survey on financing the social rented sector 1996).

The housing associations borrow on the capital market. In the past, the lenders for residential construction were predominantly institutional investors. This is not surprising, since pension funds and insurance companies have a fairly constant presence in the long-term segment of the capital market (where the life of a loan is longer than ten years). Recently, banks have also joined the investors in this sector. In addition to the investors and banks, municipalities play a (limited) role as lenders to housing associations. Moreover, the associations themselves will start to provide funds for their own sector. The associations with a surplus of assets desire to invest this in the sector itself (Spijkers, 1994). Until some time ago, the state provided loans to the associations. During the 1980s, these state loans were systematically replaced by borrowing on the capital market (Priemus, 1996). Since 1988, state loans have no longer been available (Van Hees, 1996). And the "grossing and balancing" operation also terminated the state loans that were still on the books (cf. Section 2.4).

The most prevalent kind of loans used to finance the social rented sector were annuity-based. But fixed-term loans were also used. The most common term of the loans was 30 to 40 years. The interest rates are fixed for 10 years or longer (OTB survey on financing the social rented sector 1996). The loan conditions and interest rates are favorable (thanks to the guarantees provided by the WSW and the CFV) compared to the terms common in other non-profit sectors and abroad (Spijkers, 1994; Gruis, 1996). In 1995, the average interest rate on the loans was 7.5 percent, approximately 0.25 per cent above the rate on newly issued state bonds. In some cases, loans were made by municipalities. A loan from a municipality for which it had to borrow in the capital market was approximately 15 basic points above the rate on government bonds (OTB survey on financing the social rented sector 1996).

It is customary for lenders to demand a loan guarantee from the WSW. Many lenders make additional demands on the solvency of the associations. The reason for this is that the debt ceilings used by the WSW are higher than some lenders are used to, and it also helps them to choose among the associations that apply for loans. In recent years, a number of associations seemed to be heading for financial problems, and this was the reason to apply the solvency test. The problems were averted because of government intervention, but the investors incurred losses because high-interest loans were prematurely repaid. The willingness to provide loans depends largely on the solvency of the association (the ratio of own assets to total assets, including borrowed capital). Lenders tend to use the historic cost as the basis for the valuation of the assets, whereby they apply a minimum-valuation rule. This rule stipulates that dwellings with an economic value structurally below the historic cost must be valuated on the basis of the economic value. The solvency requirements of the lenders will reflect the differences in the situations. Their requirements will be influenced by other elements in the assessment, such as the market position of the properties, the liquidity, rentability, quality of management, and the book value. An association should expect to be rated by being compared to the national average at the very least (even though the national average itself remains contentious: percentages mentioned in various sources range from 7 to 10 percent). In general, the solvency requirements where the assets are valuated on the basis of historic prices range from a minimum of 5 percent to an aspired 10 to 15 percent (Gruis, 1996).

Not all lenders impose additional conditions on the guarantees provided by the WSW. The WSW provides a guarantee until the solvency becomes negative when the valuation of the assets is based on current operating value by WSW standards or stricter ones. The solvency is higher when the total assets are valuated on the basis of current operating value rather than on the basis of historic cost, modified by the minimum-valuation rule. In principle, this allows the associations to pledge the full economic value of their assets (valuated by WSW norms) as collateral. This does, however, imply that they lose their freedom to choose among lenders on the capital

Table 2.2 The trend of annual new construction in the social rented sector compared to total new construction, 1983-1995, and the planned production 1996-1997

	Number of completed social rented dwellings	Number of completed dwellings	Share of the social rented sector (%)
1983	52,611	111,127	47
1984	49,233	112,732	44
1985	34,596	98,131	35
1986	35,770	103,330	35
1987	35,851	110,091	33
1988	40,197	118,446	34
1989	35,976	111,233	32
1990	28,449	97,384	29
1991	22,514	82,888	27
1992	25,064	86,164	29
1993	22,360	83,689	27
1994	22,431	87,369	26
1995	23,758	93,836	25
1996	20,000	-	-
1997	22,000	-	-

Source: CBS Statistics Netherlands, Maandstatistiek Bouwnijverheid (Construction statistics), March 1996.

market if they slip below the prevailing norms on the basis of historic cost. This may be detrimental to the continuity of an association (Gruis, 1996). It might also have a negative effect on the terms of loans they may need. But in the present state of the market, there are hardly any differences in the terms of loans to the associations.

The annual demand for financing is related to the volume of the new construction program. Table 2.2 shows the development trend of the construction of social rented dwellings in the Netherlands. The estimates for 1996 and 1997 do not distinguish between social rented dwellings and social homeowner dwellings.

We assume that approximately 6,000 social homeowner units will be completed annually in 1996 and 4,000 in 1997. The number completed in 1995 was 8,000. We made these estimates by extrapolating the observed trend of decline in the annual production volume of such dwellings.

The associations are expected to make a major construction effort during the next few years. The National Housing Program, compiled by the two umbrella organizations in the social rented sector, sets a target of 100,000 new inexpensive rented dwellings (a monthly rent below NLG 700 per month in 1995 prices) for the period 1996-2000 (Priemus, 1996). The total for the period until the year 2010 would amount to 217,000 dwellings. This requires an investment of approximately 30 billion guilders, of which 3.1 billion would not be cost-effective. It is expected that the associations will have to invest some 60 billion before 2010 in new construction, renovations, sustainable building, demolition, and the promotion of livability. Of that amount, some 20 billion would not be cost-effective (NCIV, 1996).

It remains to be seen, however, whether the associations will invest adequately in new dwellings. Construction subsidies to institutional investors were all but abolished in 1988. Since then, they have largely withdrawn from investing in new rented dwellings. The housing associations now find themselves in the same position as the institutional investors, as far as investment in new rented dwellings is concerned. Certainly if the long-term interest rates were to increase, a shortage of new initiatives to build new rented housing would come about (Priemus, 1995).

Another modification of the expected demand for financing would result from the increase in the sale of social rented dwellings. The associations can create gains when the sales price exceeds the book value; they will then have cash available. An increase in the sale of social rented housing would thus diminish their dependency on the capital market.

Recently, the Ministry of Housing developed a forecasting model that gives insight into the expected long-term development of the financial position of the social rented sector in the context of the investment need and rent policy. The model results in a forecast of the trend in assets accumulation in the social rented sector for the period 1995-2009, under varying conditions of rent increases, inflation, and interest rates. The forecast shows that the assets in 2009 are largely determined by the rate of rent increase, inflation, and interest rates. A sensitivity analysis shows that:

- A variation by one percent in the rent increase during the period under consideration would yield a change of the general financial reserves (ABR) in 2009 in the order of 30 billion guilders (*ceteris paribus*);
- A variation by one percent in the interest rate would change the reserves by 25 billion (*ceteris paribus*);
- A variation by one percent in the inflation rate would change the reserves by 15 billion (*ceteris paribus*).

Depending on the scenarios used in the application of the model, the total assets of the sector may vary from minus 15 billion to plus 19 billion in the year 2009 (Tommel, 1996). However, these figures are highly questionable. The main criticism of the model is that it is based on the accounting valuation rules specified by the Council for Annual Reports. Therefore, the links between investment, rent development, and the development of the assets are limited. Because the valuations in the model are based on historic costs, the future operational value of the housing stock after 2009 remains largely overlooked (cf., De Reyger, 1996).

2.6 Risk and guarantees in the social rented sector

The BBSH stipulates that the housing associations are responsible for their financial continuity. The municipalities audit their activities. The new independent status of the associations implies greater autonomy with regard to policy. The downside is that they now run risks. Therefore, they have to develop a financially prudent policy (Bouwmans, 1995). The financial resilience of the association itself is the first provision to absorb financial risks. There is an accumulation of experience and expertise in financial management within the associations (Spijkers, 1994; Priemus, 1996). Some associations, however, have wrongfully used investment derivatives. When these proved to be insecure, they lost millions of guilders within weeks (Priemus, 1996).

The financial resilience varies between associations. Housing associations experiencing financial problems have recourse to the Central Fund for Housing (CFV). The CFV is a mutual fund established by and for the associations. It is meant to support financially weak associations and, where necessary, help them to restructure their operations. To this end, each association contributes annually to the fund. The amount of the required contribution is established on the basis of the financial situation of an association (SEO, 1993). If an association does not qualify for (further) participation or guarantees from the WSW, they can appeal for help to the CFV. The CFV provides interest-free loans to such destitute associations on the condition that they can become self-supporting within three years. Sometimes this requires a restructuring of an association. In principle, the CFV contributes half the cost of such an operation. The other half is mostly borne by the municipality, which is ultimately responsible for housing (Priemus, 1996). The conditions imposed by the CFV for support closely reflect those used by the WSW in judging the creditworthiness of associations.

Between its inception in 1988 and 1995, 11 housing associations have been financially supported by the CFV to a total amount of NLG 500.4 million. The CFV anticipates that requests for assistance from the fund will increase in the future. This expectation is based on two circumstances. In the first place, the rent increases tend to be lower than the rate allowed in the "grossing and balancing" deal, especially because the rate of inflation is lower than the 3 percent anticipated at the time. Secondly, their market positions do not always allow the housing associations to impose the full rate of agreed rent increases. But even under the present rent conditions, there will be housing associations with such financial hardship that their operations would stay in the red without the support from the Fund (CFV, 1996).

Dutch housing associations can borrow with guarantees issued by municipalities or the WSW. The security provided by the WSW is linked to the purpose of the loan. The WSW can only secure loans intended to extend activities in the field of housing as specified on a limitative list of purposes. For instance, the WSW is not allowed to secure loans intended to finance general-purpose investments, participation in commercial properties, or the construction of homes for the elderly (NCIV, 1995). As of May 1, 1996 the WSW counted 620 participants and the secured assets amounted to 16 billion guilders. The expectation was that by the end of that year, the guaranteed assets would have grown to 50 billion and to 100 billion by the year 2000 (Van Hees, 1996). It should be noted that the WSW is not the only organization to provide loan guarantees. Also municipalities secure loans to associations.

If housing associations borrow with loan guarantees issued by the WSW, there is a triple guarantee. The primary security is formed by the financial resilience of the association itself and of the entire sector through the participation of the CFV. The secondary security consists of the capital assets of the WSW, which are created by a single capital contribution from the state and the fees the associations pay to obtain guarantees. The tertiary security is formed by the ultimate responsibility of the state and the municipalities which equally share this task (Van der Schaar, 1991, p. 404). The attractive interest rates on loans secured by the WSW demonstrate the great confidence that lenders have in the Fund. Their confidence is largely due to the ultimate security provided by the state (Priemus, 1995).

If a housing association wants to use the facilities of the WSW, it must register with the Fund. Before the WSW approves an application, it tests the creditworthiness of the candidate. As of 1995, the evaluation of the financial position of the associations is based on their assets. Their solvency positions must be positive to be admitted. This implies that the securities provided by the WSW to any association have to stay below a set ceiling. This amount is annually determined by the amount of the loans an association has taken out, which is subtracted from its total assets. The value of the assets is calculated as the sum of each of its housing complexes, for which the value is derived on the basis of the principles of the "grossing and balancing" agreement. That agreement stipulates an annual rent increase of at most 3.5 percent through 1999 and thereafter of at most 3 percent; an increase in annual maintenance costs of at least 3 percent, and major renovations costing NLG 15,000 (1994 price level) at least in the 25th year of operation. As far as the operating period is concerned, an economic life of at most 50 years is foreseen. For future investment needs, an interest rate of at least 7 per cent is assumed; this rate is also used to discount future income and expenses. If the real interest rates deviate from the current rate of 7 percent, yield corrections will be made (Van den Dolder, 1994). The value of the loan is then calculated by discounting future cash flows associated with the loan by the interest rate used to calculate the assets (Gruis, 1996). Meanwhile, because of the lower inflation rate than the 3 percent assumed for the "grossing and balancing" agreement, other parameters are now under review (WSW, 1994).

2.7 Opportunities for outside lenders

There are clearly opportunities in the Netherlands for activities by foreign lenders. The market for loans to housing associations in the Netherlands is wide open for foreign investors. The capital needs for investments by the housing associations will remain substantial during the next few years, amounting to 5-6 billion guilders per year (OTB survey on financing the social rented sector 1996). Thanks to the guarantees available through the WSW and the role of the CFV, loans to housing associations in the Netherlands are a safe investment. Nevertheless, this overall positive image should be seen in perspective. In the first place, sufficient financing is available for all providers of social rented housing in the Netherlands, which implies that the market for foreign lenders is limited. Mainly due to the Dutch pension system, there are institutional investors in need of investment opportunities. Yet in view of the scope of their investment portfolio, Dutch investors are not always willing to lend to social housing associations. In the second place, the very limited risks lead to a yield that is only fractionally higher than the rate paid on Dutch government bonds.

Loans to Dutch housing associations could provide an opportunity for diversification in the investment portfolio of foreign investors, possibly as an alternative to the purchase of Dutch government bonds.

3
BELGIUM

P.J. Boelhouwer

3.1 Introduction

A comparison of Western European housing systems reveals that the countries that differ most are neighbors, the Netherlands and Belgium. In the Netherlands, the social rented sector is highly developed. In contrast, the most dominant sector in the Belgian housing market is owner-occupancy. It is so strongly developed that hardly any rental dwellings can be found in Belgium's rural areas. This situation is a reflection of the Roman Catholic ideal of home ownership. A home of one's own is thought to enhance the development of citizens and the family. In this light, the Belgian government has promoted home ownership for decades; in fact, home ownership has been one of the pillars of government policy (Rietman, 1993, p. 300). Residential construction is largely left to private initiative. In principle, anyone who wants to build a house has the green light. As the old adage goes, "a Belgian is born with a brick in his belly."

A second noteworthy difference between these neighboring countries is the very small degree of direct influence that the government exercises over large segments of the housing market. As A. Martens puts it, "In Belgium, the market for potatoes is more strongly regulated than the housing market," (cited in Scheers, 1986). Strong regulation does occur in a limited area, namely the social housing market. Yet even in that sector, there is no nationwide policy, as a consequence of the regionalization of responsibilities and authority for housing. Flanders, Brussels, and Wallonia all have their own eligibility criteria and allowances in the social rented sector. They all have their own form of subsidy for construction and acquisition. Each administration has its own program of low-interest loans for large families, its own regional guarantee program, and its own allowances to cover the costs of moving and equipping the new dwelling. (See Menkveld, 1993, p. 75).

Table 3.1 gives an overview of the distribution of the dwelling stock over the tenure classes. As that table shows, the social rented sector in Belgium has remained modest in size, by European standards. It accounts for a mere 6 percent of the entire stock. For various reasons --primary among which is the sale of social rented units-- the sector has shrunk so much that it does not have enough units to accommodate low-income households. These groups thus have to take recourse to the private rented sector. There, the rents are higher even though the quality of the dwellings is lower (Goossens,

Table 3.1 The Belgian housing stock by tenure class on January 1, 1980 and 1991, percentages

	1980	1991
Owner-occupancy	59	65
Rental, of which	38	34
non-profit sector	18	18
commercial sector	82	82
Other	3	1

Source: European Commission, 1994, pp. 59-60.

1993, p. 66). The distribution of the tenure classes is very similar in the regions of Flanders and Wallonia. It should be noted, however, that over half of the housing stock in the Brussels region is in the private rented sector. While there are over 251,000 social rented dwellings in Belgium, the majority are single-family houses. Only in the region of the capital, Brussels, is the social rented sector predominantly in multi-family buildings (Van de Ven, 1995, p. 36).

3.2 The institutional structure

In Belgium, social rented dwellings have traditionally been built and operated by accredited construction firms. These contractors are public limited companies. The participants are the region, the province, and the municipality, but private shareholders are also represented on the board of directors (Gerrichhauzen and Van Giessen, 1984, p. 306). The three regional Housing Societies finance the construction of the dwellings and supervise the building activities. Their role is legally circumscribed as follows: to promote the establishment of local construction companies; to extend loans to those organizations; and to build dwellings if and when the local construction companies should prove unable to do so. In addition to the Flemish Housing Society, Flanders also has a Flemish Land Company. The task of the latter organization is to improve housing conditions in rural areas. In Wallonia and Brussels, these two organizations have merged.

The Housing Fund of the Association of Large Families in Belgium, which was founded in 1928, has been divided into three regional housing funds. These housing funds extend mortgages for the construction, purchase, and renovation of owner-occupied dwellings. In Brussels, the loans are available to families with at least two children. In Wallonia and Flanders, a family must have at least three to qualify.

Since the beginning of the present decade, Belgian law has allowed private parties to operate social rented dwellings. In Flanders, this was only possible in 1990 and 1991. Since the introduction in 1992 of an "emergency program," this option is available throughout the country. It is not the intention, however, to transfer ownership of these dwellings to private parties. The private operators are only expected to carry out certain parts of a project.

The units built by the accredited construction companies are primarily intended as rentals. In contrast to the Dutch situation, in Belgium, the (sitting) tenant has the option to purchase the dwelling. To be eligible to buy it, however, the renter cannot own another dwelling or enjoy the use of any other one. Depending on the income, the buyer may also be eligible for a one-time contribution to offset part of the purchase price. If a renter complies with the conditions, the Housing Society or the construction company cannot refuse to sell the property; the tenant thus has the right to buy. There are some exceptions to this rule, however. For instance, the companies do not have to sell if the sale would jeopardize their financial position. Furthermore, sale is not mandatory if the company would no longer be able to carry out its statutory responsibility, thereby threatening to undermine the social aims.

As pointed out earlier, the households with the lowest income levels in Belgium have to take recourse to the private rented sector, in the main. They cannot afford to buy a home of their own, while the social rented sector is often inaccessible. The reason is that the supply of social rented dwellings is very small and the waiting lists are long.

3.3 Supervision

As mentioned above, the three regional Housing Societies oversee the performance of the local construction companies. The government plays a dominant role in the Housing Societies and is directly responsible for oversight of these organizations (as elaborated below in Section 3.6). Therefore, the government ultimately guarantees all the activities that are undertaken by the diverse actors in the social rented sector in Belgium.

3.4 Subsidies for the social rented sector

Object subsidies and operating subsidies

The construction of social rented dwellings is financed by the regional Housing Societies. Until a few years ago, the financing was based on a system of interest subsidies. To find funds to provide these subsidies, the Housing Society took out loans on the capital market at the market interest rate. Incidentally, Housing Societies were required to extend loans to the accredited construction companies in the form of an annuity loan with a life of 66 years and at a low rate of interest (from 2 to 2.5 percent).

Due to the financial restrictions of the interest subsidy and the pre-financing (as elaborated below), the government and the Housing Societies can only carry out a marginal construction program. The production of new dwellings in the social sector dropped from 15,000 units in 1979 to a scant 500 dwellings in 1991. In order to reduce the housing shortage that ensued, the Flemish government made a financial injection available in 1992. They made 30 billion Belgian francs (1.7 billion Dutch guilders) available for the social rented sector to be allocated over the subsequent three years. This "emergency program" goes by the name of Domus Flandria and is focused on 15 municipalities. In 1993, 6,500 dwellings were built in the social sector. In 1994, another 7,000 were to be completed. Under this special program, production is considerably higher than in the regular program. Concretely, In Flanders, about 1,700 social rented dwellings were built in 1994 under the regular program, whereas 3,270 were built in the same year under the "emergency program." It remains to be seen what will happen when the special program is terminated. According to information from the Housing Societies, Domus Flandria is a short-lived initiative. It will only last as long as it takes to reach the target of the emergency program, which is the construction or renovation of 10,000 dwellings.

In 1975, the financial restrictions of the economic downturn gave impetus to the plan to start up a system of pre-financing in the social rented sector. In the short term, the system facilitates the construction of relatively many social rented dwellings. In the longer term, however, the accumulation of debts led to major budgetary problems in social housing provision. In the course of the regionalization process, these debts were transferred to the three regional administrations. Unfortunately, the regions were not allocated any extra financial means to service the debts. Not surprisingly, investments in the social rented sector have declined dramatically since 1981. As a consequence, the local companies undertook a lower volume of new construction jobs. The origin of the debt crisis may be sketched as follows. The National Housing Society (NHM) was obliged to extend low-interest long-term (66 years) loans to the accredited construction companies. Yet the NMH had financed all these loans on the capital market with loans that had a relatively short life. In Flanders, the usual term for a loan is about eight years. Every eight years, the outstanding obligations thus had to be refinanced at current interest rates. In this way, the high interest rates prevailing in the seventies and eighties generated heavy financial obligations on the capital market. Subsequently, hefty subsidies were needed not only for new dwellings but also for existing ones.

In all three regions, the system of pre-financing has been abandoned. Instead, the regions use annual budget credits. Each year, the region makes funds available according to a given budget. These budgets have to be sufficient for the needs of the Housing Societies, the Land Companies, and the Housing Funds. It should be noted that Wallonia and Brussels subsidize very few dwellings through this facility.

The available budget is based on an article in the budget of the Ministry of Public Works. For that reason, that budget is called the National Housing Fund. The Flemish Housing Society (VFM) indicated that in 1995, 69 percent of the annual investment program in Flanders consisted of direct subsidies from the region. The remaining 31 percent was supposed to be borrowed on the capital market by the Housing Society. The total proportion of object subsidies provided per social rented dwelling was estimated by the Belgian government in 1993 to run between 60 and 100 percent of the construction costs. The precise figure would depend on which subsidy program was applied (European Commission, 1993, p. 96).

In Flanders, there was some experimentation with the alternative financing system between 1990 and 1991 in the designated housing shortage areas. The intent of this regulation was to draw private initiative into the construction and operation of rental dwellings for lower-income groups. For each dwelling, the government awarded a one-time basic grant in the amount of 265,000 francs to the builder. The rental units could be built by the accredited construction companies or by private organizations or individuals. In addition to the building grant (made to the principal), there was also a provision for rent compensation. The landlord was allowed to charge a certain amount in rent. The rent compensation represented the difference between the amount owed by the tenant in light of his income, on the one hand, and the set amount that the landlord had a right to charge, on the other. At most, rent compensation could run 5,000 francs per month (as of 1990, this amount was indexed each year).

In 1991, this experiment with alternative financing came to a halt. The system proved to have too little effect. Moreover, it required a great deal of administration. Finally, it was not feasible to check the income of the tenant, whereby the system proved to be ineffectual.

In its most recent policy paper, the Flemish Ministry of Housing proposes a new financing system for social housing in Flanders (De Batselier, 1994). It would eventually replace the old system of pre-financing. The proposal revolves around two points:

1. The VHM takes out loans on the capital market to cover the investment programs, with the option to arrange interim financing. The maximum term of the loans is 27 years. During that period, the region takes an intermediate position by way of a regressive interest subsidy (for instance, 100 percent over 15 years, 50 percent over the subsequent six years, and so forth).
2. The VHM then turns around and lends these funds to the local Housing Societies. This is done in two steps: the investment phase and the consolidation phase. The investment phase lasts two years at most, and the interest is four percent. The maximum amount is 100 percent of the cost price. The consolidation phase lasts at most 33 years, which is half the time stipulated in the old system. The maximum amount is 100 percent of the cost price, increased by the financial obligations incurred during the period of investment. The repayment during the consolidation phase will take place through progressive annuities (2.5 percent the first two years, after which the annuity rises by three percent).

The aim of this interest subsidy system is to pave the way for a self-supporting system of financing. In this way, the VHM can play a more dynamic role and accumulate capital of its own that can be used for social housing. It is not yet known when this system will be introduced.

The self-supporting system of financing also has a disadvantage: the local societies are sensitive to the income position of their renters. It is assumed that the accredited companies should be able to generate rental revenues amounting to 3.25 percent of the book value of their properties (Van de Ven, 1995, p. 43).

Rent subsidy and rent-setting
Unlike the Netherlands, Belgium does not have a system of individual rent allowances. Subsidies in the social rented sector are provided through a system of individual rent calculations. In that system, the amount of rent due is dependent on the household's income. Only occupants of dwellings that are owned by companies with Housing Society accreditation are eligible for this program. Applicants for rent subsidy also include those who leave a so-called unhealthy dwelling, have a low income, and move into a private rented unit.

The rent level is determined in three phases. The first step is to calculate the cost price (brought up to date). The next step is to calculate the basic rent. The last step is to calculate the real rent, which is the amount the occupant actually pays. This real rent is the individual calculated rent. Though differences exist between the regions in the way the real rent is determined, the procedure is broadly similar. (For a discussion of the regional differences, see Papa, 1992, p. 36.)

A tenant whose income subsequently rises in excess of the maximum amount allowed can continue to live in the dwelling. However, in Flanders, the landlord can terminate the lease if the tenant's income is higher than the amount that would call for charging twice the basic rent.

Flanders and Wallonia review the basic rent annually, thus bringing the real rent up to date. The real rent can then be raised or lowered. In Brussels, individual rent calculation takes place once every two years.

After renovation, the updated cost price often rises. Furthermore, a rent hike may occur in midyear. Rents might also be adjusted when there is a sudden and dramatic change in the tenant's financial situation. The change may be brought about by the death or retirement of the tenant or his/her spouse, by the departure or arrival of a wage-earning family member, or by a decline in income of at least 20 percent over three consecutive months.

The local companies have to dip into their own funds to make up the difference between the basic rent and the contract (or real) rent (NEI, 1989). When the tenant's income is relatively high, the real rent can also turn out to be higher than the basic rent, according to this method of calculating the rent. By the high and low real rents obtained in this fashion, the companies should come out even financially.

Unlike the situation in other countries, the Belgian government does not transfer the difference between the updated cost price and the real rent to the companies in the form of a subsidy. The companies are supposed to absorb the differences within their own budgets. They are able to do so in part because of the interest subsidies provided by the government. In addition, all three regions give a discount for children in the household; the lower rent revenues are directly reimbursed by the government.

There are two reasons why the Belgian rent system is financially viable. First, the maximum income ceiling for occupants of social rented dwellings is fairly high. During the 1970s, it proved that nearly 75 percent of all Belgian households fell into this income category. In the meantime, the ceiling has been lowered somewhat. Nevertheless, the number of people who are eligible for social housing is very large.

The second explanation for the viability of the rent system is that the companies are very tolerant of households whose income has risen after taking occupancy of a social rented dwelling. When the increase has been extreme, these households may be forced to move. But the companies prefer to adjust the rent. Thus, as a consequence of their financial independence, the companies do not serve the lowest income groups exclusively. Moreover, this group is confronted with stiff competition for housing --the stock of social rented dwellings is already small-- from middle-class households and households with higher incomes (Wiktorin, 1992, p. 20; Van de Ven, 1995, pp. 43-45).

3.5 Financing in the social rented sector

The previous section touched upon the means of financing as part of the discussion of object subsidies in Belgium. It was pointed out that individual construction companies do not take out loans on the capital market. The loans are arranged by the three regional Housing Societies. In the OTB survey on financing in the social rented sector, conducted in 1996, the Flemish Housing Society indicated that direct financing by way of the private capital market is highly unusual. In 1995, only one dossier was financed in this manner. In this regard, the informants remarked that it is virtually impossible for individual construction companies to obtain outside assets on their own accord. The only ones that are able to do so have a very strong financial position. Regardless of the feasibility, there is really hardly any need to look for outside assets in Belgium, because the regional Housing Societies take care of the financing. Part of the financing costs are, however, covered by the construction companies' own assets. At present, this coverage is estimated at roughly 21 percent in Flanders and five percent in Wallonia (OTB survey, 1996). Of course, wide differences may arise between individual construction companies and specific projects. For Flanders, we can identify which financial institutions were involved in financing of the social rented sector in 1995. Data from the OTB survey reveal that distribution to be as follows:

- Directly from the capital market: 0.3%
- Via the Flemish Housing Society: 30.7%
- Via the region (object subsidies):   20.8%
- Via construction companies (own assets):   20.0%
- Via the emergency program Domus Flandria: 27.6%

Van den Cruyce and Van Dender (1993, pp. 75-94) give an overview of the way financing by the regional Housing Societies is arranged on the capital market. In the 1980s, the former NMH still provided long-term public loans at coupon interest rates to institutional investors as well as private individuals. This form of long-term financing has come to an end for various reasons, including changes in the financial markets. In the past, institutional investors were interested in long-term investments at a fixed rate of interest. For several years now, the Housing Societies have had to take up the money under the conditions prevailing on the market. These loans were closed after making a proposal in which the regional Housing Society gave guidelines for the life of the loan, the interest rate, and the stipulations on repayment of the loan. In general, the preferred method is to issue bonds, which implies that capital is paid back at the end of the term of the loan. On the basis of the proposals sent in by the financial institutions, the Housing Society makes a motivated offer and submits it to the Financial Administration. This department, in turn, approaches an outside consultant for advice. In view of the continually fluctuating interest rates, this entire procedure has to be carried out in two working days. Furthermore, a request must be sent to the regional government for permission to take out the loan.

Until recently, the regional government was somewhat hesitant to use new financial techniques, such as BIBOR interest. BIBOR stands for Belgian Interbank Office Rate. When taking out a loan of this type, the borrower has the option to switch to a fixed interest rate loan after three, six, or nine months. That option can be exercised at a price, however; in that event, one pays more than the market interest rate. This is a way to speculate on declining interest rates.

The Housing Societies try to arrange for as much variety as possible in closing the loans. Within one and the same loan approval, the variety allows for a number of loans at a fixed interest rate, a number with a periodically adjustable rate, and a number at BIBOR interest rates. One example is the loans arranged in 1995 by the VHM. The VHM floated two major loans, with a view to supplementary financing by the loans that were approved by the Flanders Region. These two loans were floated under the following conditions:
1) a ten-year loan with a fixed interest rate of 7.14 percent;
2) a roll-over credit (from BIBOR flat rate).

The difference between the interest rates on government loans and loans to the VHM is negligible. The surcharge on a loan with a life of ten years at a fixed rate of interest amounts to a mere 0.14 percent. This amount is added to the OLO flat rate that the Region owes. The BIBOR flat rate applies to roll-over credit. In 1995, inflation in Belgium was running at about 2.0 percent. Thus, the real interest rate is low, running at approximately 5.1 percent.

Whereas loans could previously be arranged with institutional investors, this is virtually impossible now, even though investors are willing to make long-term investments. The reason given by Van den Cruyce and Van Dender (1993, p. 76) is that the Region's guarantee is based on a lower estimate than the State's guarantee. As a consequence of this discrepancy, the loans made to Housing Societies are less interesting to the institutional investors. According to these authors, there is also a discrepancy between the financing opportunities that are actually used and the opportunities available on the market. To break this impasse, the possibility is being considered to approach the institutional investors through the financial institutions. The latter would then provide a financial service in exchange for a given commission. However, in view of the overload of administrative activities, the Housing Societies cannot take on this task yet.

The loans floated by the VHM are exclusively annuity loans. The interest rate is often adjusted during the life of the loan. The usual term for which the loan is extended ranges from seven to 12 years. The loans to which the VHM obligates itself are guaranteed by the Flanders Region for 90 percent.

As pointed out in the previous section, the "emergency program" known as Domus Flandria got started in 1992. In this public holding company, which is in the form of a public limited company, the Housing Societies own half plus one of the shares. The holding is authorized to arrange for mortgages on the capital market; these mortgages are guaranteed by the regions. The State sets a maximum on the amounts that may be borrowed. Besides loans, the participants also bring in their own financial means. The initiative may be taken by construction companies as well as by private parties. Half of the capital in the holding is brought in by private investors, primarily banks. The other half of the capital is brought in by the Regional Investment Society for Flanders and by the VHM. The investors receive an interest subsidy from the region. In addition, rent subsidies are made widely available. In this way, an effort is made to prevent a large number of dwellings from being rented to high-income groups, as was common up to that time. The reason to do so is to make sure the rents cover the costs of operating rental housing.

The annual demand for financing in Belgium's social rented sector is closely tied to the volume of the new construction program (Table 3.2).

As Table 3.2 shows, the production of social rented dwellings in Belgium has been extremely volatile over the past decades. Up till 1980, the number of social rented dwellings increased annually by an average of eight to ten thousand. Meanwhile, about 2,500 dwellings were sold each year. Since 1981, the production of social rented units has declined dramatically. The share of social rented dwellings has been no more than

Table 3.2 **Development in annual new construction activities in the social rented sector compared with the total number of housing starts in Belgium 1980-1995 and projected production 1996-1997**

	Number of starts social rented units	Number of housing starts	Share of social rented dwellings (%)
1980	10,300	48,600	21
1985	700	30,000	2
1986	530	24,000	2
1987	900	29,300	3
1988	660	33,000	2
1989	1,200	44,400	3
1990	1,200	41,100	3
1991	500	44,500	1
1992	750	46,600	2
1993	10,100	43,700	23
1994	3,000	-	-
1995	3,300	-	-
1996	2,600	-	-
1997	2,700	-	-

Source: NMH, 1988; European Commission, 1994; OTB survey on financing in the social rented sector, 1996.

five percent of the total housing production since 1986. In 1988, for the first time, there was even a decline in the number of social rented dwellings, in balance. At that point, the number of sales exceeded the new production (Boelhouwer and Van der Heijden, 1992, p. 84). As mentioned earlier, the new construction in Flanders has picked up since 1992 because of the emergency program Domus Flandria. For instance, the production of social rented dwellings in Belgium peaked in 1993, when 10,000 new units were built. The program seemed to be terminated in 1994, however. For that reason, the total number of social rented dwellings in Belgium fell back to the usual low level, hovering around 3,000 units per year. The lion's share of this production takes place in Flanders. The annual production in Wallonia is a mere 400-450 dwellings. In the Brussels region, the 1995 production amounted to 485 units, whereas the production in other years was running about 100 dwellings. In 1995, the average initial costs of social rented units varied across the three regions. The differences are slight between Flanders and Wallonia; the average initial construction cost in Flanders was BF 2,750,000 (or NLG 151,250), while it was BF 2,607,267 (or NLG 143,340) in Wallonia (both figures in 1993 prices). The region of the capital, Brussels, has a somewhat higher figure: BF 4,000,000 (or NLG 220,000) (OTB survey on financing in the social rented sector, 1996). We may assume that the production of 3,000 social rented dwellings would be financed by loans taken out by the Housing Societies on the capital market. This would represent a financing demand of 57 percent (the remainder consists of equity and subsidies). Furthermore, the initial construction costs of a dwelling would run NLG 150,000 on average. Under these assumptions, the annual financing demand would be approximately NLG 257 million. In this calculation, we do not take the financing of maintenance and improvement activities into account.

3.6 Risk and guarantees in the social rented sector

As discussed above, the production and operation of housing in the social rented sector in Belgium are carried out by construction companies. These companies are relatively independent. They have a board of directors, a director, and the authority to hire personnel. The three Housing Societies provide financial, technical, administrative, and social oversight. In brief, they act as banker and supervisor. In this function, the Housing Society monitors the financial stability and health of the local construction company. If the construction companies run into financial trouble, they can count on the support of the regional Housing Societies. Incidentally, financial problems are highly exceptional for a construction company in Flanders. If problems do occur, the company can appeal to the VHM for a restructuring loan. The VHM estimates that over the past several years, between one and five percent of the construction companies had financial difficulties. Similar percentages are estimated for the region of Wallonia. Only the Brussels region has a share higher than five percent (OTB survey on financing in the social rented sector, 1996). According to the informants at the regional Housing Societies, the financial management of the construction companies is not yet mature. In Flanders and Brussels, for example, financial management lies somewhere in between being primarily a bookkeeping activity and being fully integrated, along with risk analysis, in the management of the entire organization. Management in Wallonia, in contrast, is mainly a bookkeeping activity (OTB survey on financing in the social rented sector, 1996).

The Housing Societies are private limited companies with shares similar to those issued by a public limited company and are run by a board of directors. This board is appointed by the Annual General Meeting, in which the shareholders (the region and the provinces) have a seat. The Housing Societies are supervised by the regional Ministers of Finance and Housing. In practice, the supervision is carried out by two regional commissioners, who are nominated for appointment by those ministers. The commissioners attend the meetings of the board of directors in their capacity as advisors.

As far as we know, there are no instances of construction companies that are in financial trouble. The way in which the operation of the social rented sector is organized gives little reason to expect financial difficulties. It is the Housing Societies rather than the construction companies that carry the risks entailed by refinancing the loans.

3.7 Opportunities for outside lenders

In light of the above overview, we may conclude that Belgium offers limited opportunities for outside lenders to extend loans to social landlords. We draw this conclusion despite the fact that the social rented sector in Belgium is stable and is not confronted with major problems such as vacancy or other financial setbacks. The low level of opportunity is primarily due to the extremely low level of production of social rented dwellings. With roughly 3,000 dwellings per year, the number of completions in Belgium is among the lowest in Western Europe. Subsequently, nearly half of the required financing is covered by the construction companies' own assets and the government subsidies, combined. Moreover, it is almost only possible to extend loans to the three regional Housing Societies. This makes the risk that the lenders bear extremely low. The reason is that these Societies are covered financially by the regional governments. The slight risk also keeps the interest rates extremely low. They are only about 0.14 percent higher than the level for regional loans.

4
ENGLAND

M. Oxley

4.1 Introduction

The housing stock in England can be divided into owner-occupation and three main categories of renting. The data is shown in Table 4.1. Housing association and local authority dwellings together constitute the social rented sector. Private rented housing is owned by a variety of landlords, ranging from large institutions to single individuals.

Owner-occupation has grown from around 58 percent of the stock in 1981 to nearly 67 percent in 1994. Tax relief on mortgages, despite some restrictions on their value, particularly since 1988, continues to support the sector. Home ownership has received an additional boost from the "Right to Buy" (RTB), which has switched houses from local authority control into owner-occupation.

Private rented housing remains a very small sector in England despite government efforts to revive it. This has involved the freeing up of rents and short-term letting contracts, which have predominated for new lettings since 1988.

Social rented housing comprises housing association and local authority dwellings. Since 1979 the government has reduced the significance of local authority housing by the RTB and by limiting permissions to borrow money for new development.

Table 4.1 Housing tenure in England

	1,000s dwellings	1981 % of stock	1,000s dwellings	1994 % of stock
Owner-occupied	10499	58.2	13664	67.6
Private rental	2044	11.3	2056	10.2
Housing association	422	2.3	834	4.1
Local authority	5061	28.1	3661	18.1
All dwellings	18025	100	20215	100

Source: Wilcox (1995), Tables 16a and 16b, pp. 92-93.

Housing associations are now the main developers of social housing. The sector is growing as a result of both new development and transfers of stock from local authorities. Both of these activities require finance. There is an increasing emphasis on the role of private finance in promoting these activities.

4.2 The institutional structure

Social housing in England has been dominated by local authorities who once received large subsidies to assist in their provision of dwellings. That role has, however, diminished considerably. From managing 28 percent of the total housing stock in 1981, their position changed so that by 1994 they managed only 18 percent of the stock. Since 1988 the government has made it clear that it wishes local authorities not to be housing providers but to be "strategic enablers." The enabling role means that authorities oversee and monitor housing provision in their area, working particularly with housing associations, but do not get involved significantly in new developments (Bramley, 1993).

Over the same time period, housing associations increased their share from 2.3 percent to 4.1 percent of the stock, and this is expected to continue to grow. Housing associations are non-profit organizations which are managed by voluntary committees.

Housing associations had their origins over 150 years ago in charitable housing trusts associated with industrial philanthropists (Gibb and Munro, 1991, p. 107). In the first half of this century they relied on private charitable funding and loans from local authorities. The "voluntary" nature of housing associations refers to their management by voluntary unpaid committee members. The professional staff which manage and oversee development are responsible to the management committee. From 1964 to 1988 housing associations were highly dependent on private finance in the form of generous subsidies. They tended to be classified in many quarters, in this period, as part of the public sector. Yet strictly speaking, as they were and are legally independent voluntary organizations, they are not of the public sector. Since 1988, with an increasing reliance on private finance as a result of policy changes, the government has encouraged the view that they are part of an "independent" rented sector.

Most housing associations are registered as charities and obtain the financial concessions that go with this status. This means they are treated much more favorably than the true independent landlords in the private rented sector.

UK housing associations are small by European standards. The average number of dwellings managed in 1993 was 287. This compared with 2,342 in the Netherlands and 4,755 in France (European Commission, 1993, p. 38).

Development is concentrated in the hands of the largest housing associations. Their role in providing new social housing is now crucial to the expansion of the social rented housing stock. The "umbrella organization" for housing associations is the National Housing Federation (NHF). This provides an advice, information and research role but principally a lobbying and liaison role. The NHF represents the interests of housing associations in the political arena. It also provides an important role in discussing changes in procedures with the Housing Corporation.

The Right to Buy introduced in the 1980 Housing Act has played a major part in reducing the significance of the council housing stock. Since 1980, over 1.2 million council dwellings have been sold at generous discounts to existing tenants under the Right to Buy. Some of the best quality housing has been sold and lower-income tenants are left in lower-quality stock. The process of "residualization" has left council housing with a strong welfare role to perform and very limited resources to fulfil this function adequately. Housing associations are affected to a much more limited extent by the Right to Buy. In 1994, 43,116 local authority dwellings were sold under these provisions; in the same year, 831 housing association dwellings were sold (Wilcox, 1995).

This may change in the future with the introduction of voluntary purchase grant (VPG). The details of the scheme are still being discussed but grants will be available to housing associations to encourage tenant purchases. From 1997/98, housing associations will have to offer VPG to tenants of all new schemes in order to qualify for a Housing Corporation development grant (Housing Association Weekly, 1996). Housing associations estimate they could sell 2,000 homes under the scheme.

Significant transfers of dwellings from local authorities to local housing associations are also occurring. Large Scale Voluntary Transfers (LSVT) have to be privately financed.

The finance for RTB comes mainly in the form of mortgages from building societies. As this is strictly money for expanding owner-occupation, this is not considered further in this chapter. However, the financing of LSVT is related to the continuing provision of social rented housing. This will, therefore, be considered.

Given that private finance is related principally to the development activities of housing associations, and transfers to housing associations, the emphasis of the rest of this chapter is on housing associations rather than local authorities.

4.3 Supervision

The supervision and monitoring of housing associations in England is, primarily, the responsibility of the Housing Corporation.

The current version of the housing association movement started with the formation of the Housing Corporation in 1964. The Corporation had the responsibility of promoting and overseeing housing associations. It was able to lend public money for the provisions of housing at cost-rent and for co-ownership housing. The most significant development came with the passing of the Housing Act (1974). This resulted in a major growth in housing association activities. The Housing Corporation's powers were extended and a new system of loans and grants was introduced. The money made available to the Corporation by central government was greatly increased. Since 1988, with the housing associations taking on the major role as providers of new social housing and with an increased expectation of private funding supporting their activities, the role of the Corporation has again expanded. The mission of the Housing Corporation is "to support social housing in England by working with housing associations and others to provide good homes for those in housing need" (Housing Corporation, 1994, p. 1).

The Corporation monitors the performance of housing associations, allocates public money, and promotes the development of associations. There is much emphasis on value for money: "The need to ensure that the resources allocated to us are used in the most cost effective way possible is central to all our activities." Also, "The Corporation has played an important role in promoting the housing association sector to private sector lenders" (Housing Corporation, 1994, p. 2). The Corporation is concerned with management cost efficiency: "We believe it is crucial that tenants, local authorities, lenders and others with an interest in associations' work are able to have information in order to assess and compare performance. An agreement has been reached between the Audit Commission (a government body with responsibilities for ensuring that public money is well spent) to draw up an annual program of reviews and studies to promote value for money. Performance indicators "are an invaluable part of our regulatory armoury; the information they convey - along with a wealth of other data - is then fed into our investment mechanism to ensure that we are funding efficient, effective associations who provide an excellent value for money service to their tenants" (Housing Corporation, 1994, p. 5).

The Corporation carries out its regulatory role to protect public funds, ensure a good service to tenants, and to "preserve the reputation of associations for sound management and financial strength so as to continue attracting private, unguaranteed lending from financial institutions" (Housing Corporation, 1994, p. 11).

A new system of regulation has been introduced which starts with an annual "desk top review" (DTR). This review is based on a return from associations supplemented by existing information held by the Corporation and the views of local authorities and tenants. There are periodic performance review visits to validate the information supplied by DTR and investigatory visits to address any potential concerns shown up by the review. This new system is intended to cover all associations by 1996/7.

In 1992 the Corporation introduced a system of collecting quarterly financial returns from some 600 associations - mostly those involved in development activity. This system is continuing to evolve. A system of financial forecasting is in operation to help spot potential financial problems early and to feed into the Performance and Investment Summary (PAIS), which is used to decide which associations should received capital funding. Funding is withheld from associations that perform poorly. For some associations, funding is conditional on addressing performance review concerns.

It has been argued that "despite changes in the monitoring of associations, the process of assessing financial viability still concentrates only on ratios, such as loan to asset cover. The actual terms and conditions of the loans, the suitability of the loan profile and so on, are not factors that financial viability assessments pick up formally. Informally, however, financial instruments may be the subject of discussion" (Pryke and Whitehead, 1995 p. 19).

Registration with the Housing Corporation is essential if a housing association is to receive public support. There are 2,276 housing associations registered with the Housing Corporation. Of these, 1,337 are industrial and provident societies, 675 are charitable trusts, and 264 are charitable companies limited by guarantee. There is a separate regulatory framework for each corporate status and there are two for charitable companies limited by guarantee. This means that there is regulation by the Registry of Friendly Societies, Companies House and the Charity Commission, as well as the Housing Corporation. In the report of an inquiry into Housing Association Governance, the National Federation of Housing Associations (NFHA, 1995) suggested that this additional regulation added little value to the much more rigorous regulation of the Housing Corporation. It therefore recommended that all housing associations registered with the Housing Corporation be exempt from the routine regulation of whichever body oversees their current status. The government has yet to respond to this suggestion.

4.4 Subsidies for the social rented sector

Object subsidies and development

Government policy generally has had a significant impact on housing production. It has, in particular, influenced the volume of housing completions in each sector which are shown on Table 4.2. Financial controls and the provision of subsidies have been important influences on the changes between 1980 and 1994 in Table 2.

Public sector housing, dominated by local authority or council house production, comprised about one-third of all housing completions in 1980 but by 1994 was less than 1 percent of housebuilding. This reduction was a consequence of government controls on public expenditure. Local authorities submit annual Housing Investment Programmes (HIP) to central government. These statements set out a strategy for housing development and improvement based on a review of housing conditions in the locality.

Table 4.2 Housing completions in England

	Number	1980 % of total	Number	1994 % of total
Local authorities	67337	32.9	1086	0.7
New Towns	6973	3.4	0	0
Government departments	525	0.3	16	-
Total public sector	74835	36.6	1102	0.7
Housing associations	19299	9.5	30462	20.3
Private sector	110232	53.9	118979	79
All dwellings	204366	100	150543	100

Source: Wilcox (1995), p. 97.

The Department of the Environment, which is the central government ministry responsible for housing, reviews the bids for the use of resources in the HIP statements and allocates permissions to borrow and spend on housing-related activities. By cutting back on permissions to borrow money for housing development by local authorities, central government has brought about a massive reduction in the building of council houses.

The main route for subsidies to council housing has been through central government contributions to local authorities' Housing Revenue Accounts (HRA). All current costs and payments related to the ongoing provision of council housing pass through this account. Each local housing authority has an HRA. The costs of financing debt and maintenance and management expenses are paid from this account. The income to the account includes rent and subsidies. Since 1980, subsidies have progressively been cut and rents have been increased.

The growth of housing associations has been encouraged principally by means of Housing Association Grant (HAG). This is the main object subsidy promoting social housing development. HAG is a lump-sum capital grant which was introduced in 1974. There have, however, been several revisions to the way it is calculated and the conditions governing the distribution of HAG to housing associations.

In 1974, HAG was connected with the application to housing associations of "fair rents." These were set by rent officers. For potential new schemes, the income from fair rents was calculated. The likely annual costs of management and maintenance were estimated. The income remaining after these costs had been met would be available to meet loan charges on borrowed money. This remainder would inevitably service only a small loan. The rest of the capital cost of the project was met by a grant in the form of HAG. The system was generous and HAG could in many cases meet over 70 percent of the costs.

With rising rents, a lump-sum capital grant allowed some schemes to move into surplus within a few years. In 1980 associations were required to keep a Grant Redemption Fund (GRF) into which surpluses on HAG-related schemes were paid. Central government could require that money from the GRF was used for major repairs. It could also take back money from this account.

By 1988 HAG was meeting 80 to 90 percent of the cost of the schemes. Housing associations were as a result of the 1988 Housing Act, required to issue assured tenancies at new higher rents for new developments and re-lets. This was intended to reduce HAG rates and promote more private finance. In the new system, the cost of provision, rather than the rental income, is the starting point for calculating HAG. Average HAG rates have fallen from 75 percent in 1989 to 55 percent in 1995/6.

Central to Housing Corporation funding is the Approved Development Program (ADP), which is arranged each year by the Secretary of State for the Environment following the national Budget statement. The overall size of the ADP is influenced by the estimate of need for social housing and the policy priorities of the government, local housing strategies, which are the responsibility of local housing authorities, and the level of national resources available. Allocations of the ADP to specific schemes are influenced by the government's priorities and targets, local housing needs, and value for money.

ADP investment is supplemented by a variety of other funding sources, such as free or discounted land from local authorities, and other forms of public subsidy, such as City Challenge (which is related to urban improvements). In 1994/5 over £1 billion of private finance was raised by housing associations to support the ADP. This represented, on average, 44 percent of an ADP-funded total scheme cost.

For 1996/7 the Housing Corporation's ADP investment is planned to be £31,062.8m. Of this, some £787m is planned to be spent on projects for rent, and £259m on home ownership initiatives, including the new Voluntary Purchase Grant Scheme. ADP-subsidized output in 1996/7 is forecast to total 43,000 lettings (Housing Corporation, 1996a). Over 500 housing associations will receive funding allocations.

Larger associations (owning over 2,500 dwellings) get 57 percent of the new funding, with small associations (less than 500 dwellings) getting 9 percent. It is forecast that an additional 18,100 lettings will result from non-ADP funded schemes. This includes 11,000 lettings from local authority HAG, whereby local authorities contribute to housing associations from their resources.

The government wishes to see the ADP make a substantial contribution to regeneration. For 1996/97, at least 50 percent of ADP grants should contribute to regeneration objectives. This may include housing on sites previously in residential, industrial or commercial uses, projects in designated renewal areas and on local authority estates.

Estimates of the need for new social housing calculated by the Department of the Environment (DOE) suggest that about 100,000 new social rented dwellings a year are required to meet needs that cannot be met by other means. This is the upper range of the estimate. The lower range is 60,000 dwellings per annum. The figures include no target for reducing the level of unmet needs outstanding in 1991, the base year of the assessment. Actual provision may reach the lower range of the estimate. Given the unmet needs and the probability of the upper estimate being more realistic, it has been concluded that "...the formal DOE assessment of housing needs can only be taken as confirmation that on current policies the housing shortage in England will worsen in the coming years" (Wilcox, 1995, p. 69).

Rent subsidies and rent-setting policy
Until 1989, housing association rents were set externally by the independent rent officer service. Since then, for new lettings, associations have set their own rents. For tenants who were in their dwellings before 1989, "fair rents" -- set by the rent officer and reviewed every two years -- still apply (Aughton and Malpass, 1994).

For new lets the rents are supposed, according to the government, to be affordable for tenants on low incomes. The government, however, has not defined affordability and there is an ongoing debate about what it really means. The National Federation of Housing Associations monitors rents and produces detailed information on the relationship between rents and incomes. It has suggested that "Rents are affordable if the majority of working households taking up new tenancies are not caught in the poverty trap (because of dependency on housing benefit) or paying more than 25 percent of their net income on rent." (Housing Associations Weekly,

Table 4.3 Housing association rents in England

	1980		1989		1994	
	£ per week	% of average male earnings	£ per week	% of average male earnings	£ per week	% of average male earnings
Fair rents	12.52	11.2	26.82	12.2	41.38	14.6
Assured rents			24.5	11.2	45.9	16.2

Source: Wilcox (1995).

21 January 1994, quoted in Aughton and Malpass, 1994). Over 70 percent of new assured tenants are paying rents above the affordable level on this definition.

Rent levels have risen substantially. As the information in Table 4.3 shows, housing association rents as a percentage of average male earnings rose from 11.2 percent to 16.2 percent from 1989 to 1994. The average assured rent in 1994 was £45.90 per week.

The cost of rental payments is heavily supported by housing benefits. Housing benefits are housing allowances which depend on rental costs, household income, and the size of household. The number of housing benefit recipients and the total housing benefit bill are rising rapidly. In May 1992, 340,000 housing association tenants received benefits, by November 1994 the figure was 556,000. The overall average weekly rent for housing association tenants in May 1994 was £43.60 and the average housing benefit payment was £39.50. Thus a very high proportion of gross rents was being met by housing benefits.

The government has changed the rules on housing benefits many times in an attempt to limit the rising exchequer cost. The latest change means that rents in excess of "local reference rents" will only be 50 percent eligible for housing benefit. These rents are based on averages in the private rented sector. Some dwellings are excluded: for example, housing association lettings where care and support is provided for residents. The changes came into operation in January 1996. Their effects have yet to be assessed.

4.5 Financing housing associations

The role of the ADP and HAG in the financing of housing associations was outlined in Section 4. The provision of subsidies through this system has been considerably modified since 1988 and associations are expected to raise significant sums of money for development from private sources. The transfer of housing from local authorities to housing associations was discussed in Section 2. The emphasis in this section will be on the role of private finance in promoting development and transfers. Attention will be given to the possibility of refinancing existing debt. There are, furthermore, significant changes in the pipeline which will bring about new possibilities for private finance. The two major changes are the evolution of "housing companies" and the introduction of housing investment trusts (HIT). Some comments will be made on each of these.

The 1988 Housing Act set the framework for bringing private funding into social housing development. "Mixed Funding" schemes, where public grant and private finance combine to finance development, are now the norm. Private finance is now essential to the social housebuilding program. Between £10 billion and £11 billion in private finance has been raised since 1988. As the chief executive of the Housing Corporation, Anthony Mayor, said recently, "The 1988 Housing Act has been a means to lead the rest of Europe in getting private finance and using that expenditure to its best effect. Housing associations have been able to do that without losing their basic voluntary caring ethos." (Housing Associations Weekly, 1996b).

Private finance supports several types of developments financed through the Housing Corporation's ADP where a supplement to central government spending is required. These include schemes which are classified as Mixed Funded Rent, Mixed Funded Sales, Do-it-Yourself Shared Ownership (DIYSO), and Special Needs Housing. Private finance also helps to support schemes involving Local Authority Housing Association Grant (LAHAG). These are transactions where central government funding is paid by the Housing Corporation to registered housing associations, who, in turn, reimburse local authorities for loans. This Housing Corporation expenditure is outside of the ADP cash limit.

The Large Scale Voluntary Transfers (LSVTs), where local authority stock is transferred to an existing or a new registered housing association, are 100 percent debt-financed by the private sector.

Between 1988 and 1995, over 171,000 dwellings were transferred under LSVT to housing associations set up by local authorities. In the same period, about 6,000 were transferred to existing housing associations or specially created subsidiaries of existing groups. Several housing associations also have "trickle transfer" arrangements whereby they take over homes as tenants move out. Over 17 percent of the total stock of housing association dwellings has come from transfers. This is nearly as much as the increase in the stock through development (Voluntary Housing, 1995). The executive director of the financial institution UBS Ltd has stated that "it is becoming increasingly evident to funders that lending to LSVTs represents a sound and safe investment generating a reasonable rate of return. The on-going need for good quality housing at affordable rents is undisputed and the stability of a rental stream largely free of the vagaries of movements in property values is both attractive and comforting, notwithstanding the occasional ministerial statement on housing benefits!" (Mew, 1995).

An additional activity which requires private finance is the refinancing of loans related to the residential Business Expansion Scheme (BES). In 1988 the government announced the extension of BES to include companies renting dwellings on assured tenancies. The incentives under the scheme were to be available until 1993 (Kemp, 1993). The BES was originally introduced in 1983 to promote small businesses. It provided tax relief to investors who bought shares in BES firms and gave them exemption from capital gains tax if the shares were held for at least five years. The extension of BES to companies providing housing let on assured tenancies was intended to boost the private rented sector. There is, however, an incentive to disinvest after the minimum five-year share-holding period. Many companies thus sought a "guaranteed exit route" for investors. Housing associations have in several cases provided such an exit route by buying back property which they had originally sold to a BES company. This acquisition of property requires refinancing which is sought from the private sector. Housing associations may raise private finance to replace existing loans if this improves their financial position, including their cash flow. Private finance can also be used to refinance other loans from local authorities and the Housing Corporation. It has been shown that by refinancing, associations can sometimes reduce their repayments and free themselves of restrictive obligations to the original lender (Hayes, 1996).

The Housing Corporation prepares forecasts of the volume of private finance necessary to supplement government spending (Housing Corporation, 1996b). The forecasts to 1998/99 and the data for earlier financial years shown in Table 4.4 come from the Housing Corporation's published estimates.

The total private finance needed to complete planned programs to the end of 1998/99 is about £14 billion. This covers the Housing Corporation's Mixed Funding ADP, the Local Authority Mixed Funded Program (LAHAG), and the LSVT program. Over the period 1996/97 to 1998/99, it is estimated that a further £395 million will be required to refinance existing BES schemes. Other refinancing requirements are not estimated by the Housing Corporation and are not included in Table 4.4.

The total private finance requirement has grown enormously from £29 million in 1987/88 to £1,901 million in 1995/96. Development activity under ADP and LAHAG accounted for 46 percent of this total with 50 percent being related to LSVT. The relative significance of these major components has varied from year to year and this is likely to continue in the future. It is estimated that 68 percent of private finance in 1998/99 will support the various forms of development activity.

Table 4.4 Private finance requirement (forecasts, £million)

	1987/88	1991/92	1995/96	1996/97	1997/98	1998/99
ADP	29	145	576	852	672	692
LAHAG	0	72	304	319	289	288
LSVTs	0	708	963	398	314	315
BES	0	0	22	123	116	134
Total	29	925	1901	1693	1391	1429

Source: Housing Corporation (1996b).

The figures in Table 4.4 do not take account of additional private finance that will be required to support some new initiatives. Potentially, the most significant of these is the formation of new-style "housing companies" which get involved in the provision of social housing. The 1996 Housing Act gives the Housing Corporation the power to register new "not for profit" companies as social landlords in addition to housing associations. The local housing companies will be independent bodies established by local authorities to attract private investment for new construction and repair. The Housing Corporation reckons that £2 billion will be raised by housing companies over the next three years.

The development of local housing companies is partly a response to arguments about the need to change British practice to bring it more in line with the rest of Europe. The next step would be to change the public accounting rules so that borrowing by these new companies did not count towards the public deficit. A study by the Chartered Institute of Housing and Coopers and Lybrand considered international conventions on the measuring of government financial deficits and the ways they affect the borrowing behavior of social landlords in European countries. They concluded that British practice was different from that in many other countries and adversely affected housing investment (see Wilcox and Hawksworth, 1995; Perry, 1996). The primary measure of government deficits used elsewhere is the General Government Financial Deficit (GGFD). This has been adopted by the European Union for the purposes of the Maastricht Treaty. British practice has put much emphasis on the Public Sector Borrowing Requirement (PSBR). The GGFD includes only central and local government deficits. The PSBR also includes borrowing by public corporations. It has been argued that "The adoption of government, rather than public sector, measures of budget deficits provides the basis for understanding why it is that social housing landlords in other European countries are free to raise private finance without the kind of government borrowing controls that apply uniquely to council housing in the UK." (Wilcox and Hawksworth, 1995). If the UK switches to using GGFD as the primary measure of budget deficit, the new housing companies will operate in a less restrictive environment.

The Finance Act 1996 introduced Housing Investment Trusts (HITs). These will come into being when the London Stock Exchange has agreed the regulatory framework. HITs are designed to increase institutional investment in private rented housing (Joseph Rowntree Foundation, 1996). It will, however, be possible for housing associations and local authorities to use them as a means of gaining access to new finance. Housing Investment Trusts will have shares quoted on the stock exchange. They will be able to invest in properties acquired on or after 1 April 1996. They will get two significant tax breaks: the HIT will be chargeable for corporation tax at the small companies rate (24 percent on its rental income); and there will be no capital gains tax on its property sales (Randall, 1996). Housing associations and local authorities could transfer properties to HITs and gain the financial benefits and access to new funding from institutional investors.

4.6 Risk and guarantees for housing associations

While loans are not in a formal sense underwritten or guaranteed, the regulation by the Housing Corporation and the political support which is attached to housing associations makes the lending risk very low. As well as regulation by the Housing Corporation, housing associations benefit from government support, capital grants towards new project development costs, revenue support through the housing benefit system, and an asset base acceptable to lenders as security for loans. It has been argued that "Lenders clearly take comfort from current government support, although they recognize that this creates a political risk, as changes to the grant or benefits system may adversely affect an association's long-term ability to service its debt. Lenders now believe that fundamental changes in these areas would be politically sensitive and are therefore unlikely. Additionally, public sector capital grant is subordinated to a secured provider of private finance. This means that if a security has to be realized a lender will be repaid from proceeds of the property sale before an element of grant is recovered by the Housing Corporation." (Lopategui, 1996).

The Chairman of the Housing Corporation has stated that "The attractions for private lenders rest on a sound credit risk comprising subordinated government grant, robust cash flows and a strong track record, supervised by the Housing Corporation in its complementary role as regulator of those in whom it invests. To date no lender has ever lost money on a grant backed scheme involving a registered housing association." (Pearse, 1996). The national director of residential business for the large property firm, Chesterton, has argued that "associations are increasingly considered a safe bet and capable of taking on long term commitments against a backdrop of AAA credit-related issues, the highest rating. The Housing Corporation is also widely seen as an effective safety check against financial distress or misadministration, and housing associations are now required to produce PLC (Public Limited Company) style accounts which enable benchmarking of performance between increasingly competitive associations" (Wells, 1996). Very little own capital goes into development finance. Given that state subsidy on average meets 42 percent of costs, however, the security of the 58 percent borrowed funds is good.

Research into the attitudes of financial institutions with respect to the risks of lending to housing associations has shown that the relative attractiveness of associations and the favorable balance between risks and rewards have been major reasons why banks and building societies have moved into lending for social housing (Pryke and Whitehead, 1995).

4.7 Opportunities for outside lenders

Of the total lending to housing associations, around 40 percent comes from banks, 40 percent from building societies, and 20 percent from insurance companies and pension funds. A variety of funding mechanisms are in use: short-term development finance, long-term funding, and syndicated transactions. Deals range from a few thousand to tens of millions of pounds (Pearse, 1996). Given the variety of loans, any generalizations about their characteristics are of limited value. However, loans in 1995 were at an average rate of interest of 7.5 percent to 8.5 percent. The duration of the loans varies from a few months to 30 years.

A major specialist provider of private finance is The Housing Finance Corporation (THFC). This was established in 1987 by the Housing Corporation and the National Federation of Housing Associations. As few housing associations had the strength to issue their own debt, THFC was created as a vehicle to mediate between the associations and the capital markets. The government did not consider it appropriate to back THFC with guarantees. By 1991, THFC had raised 15 to 20 percent of the private sector funding needs of housing associations (Pryke and Whitehead, 1991). A variety of instruments have been used: zero coupon and deep discounted stock, bank loans, and stepped coupon loans. Each loan is provided with considerable cover. THFC earns fees from arranging finance packages. THFC is trying to strike a balance between building up reserves and operating within its status as a non-profit-making body. The Housing Corporation's Private Finance Survey (1995) notes that THFC has on-lent £83.8 million borrowed from individual banks via club deals to registered associations. The individual lenders include several overseas banks.

The Housing Corporation's Private Finance Survey provides a detailed ranking of lenders committed to funding in excess of £10 million. Thirty-two banks are listed, 13 institutions, and 16 building societies. There are several foreign banks in the list. The French Banque Paribas ranks fifth and Banque International de Luxembourg is ninth. The rest of the list includes several German and Japanese banks: for instance, Bayerische LB and Bayerische Vereinsbank, both in Munich; Depfa Bank and Hessische Bank Thüringen Landesbank, both in Frankfurt; and Industrial Bank of Japan, in Tokyo.

Foreign banks clearly are already significantly involved in lending to social housing in England. Given the continuing high level of demand for private finance, there are likely to be ongoing opportunities for further participation in this market. The list of institutions involved in lending is headed by THFC, and several insurance companies are included. The Nationwide and the Halifax head the UK building societies ranking. The Bradford and Bingley and Britannia building societies were ranked third and fourth in terms of the volume of committed funding to housing associations.

5
DENMARK

P.J. Boelhouwer

5.1 Introduction

In Denmark, as in Sweden, we can distinguish four housing market sectors. The largest is the owner-occupied sector (51 percent), followed by the non-profit rented sector (21 percent), the private rented sector (19 percent), and the cooperative sector (five percent) (see Table 5.1). The cooperative sector is a hybrid form of the homeowner and the non-profit rented sectors. Cooperative associations have existed in Denmark since the turn of the century, but it was only in 1980 that the sector was given forceful impetus by a change in legislation. The new law states that when private landlords sell their property, they first have to give the tenants a chance to take over the units as participants in a cooperative. Only when the tenants do not take up the offer can the complex be sold to third parties. Another way to create cooperatives is by building them new (Van de Ven, 1995, p. 135). The Danish housing market is also characterized by the large share of second homes in the stock. A rising number of households have an income that would permit them to buy one. It is estimated that roughly 10 percent of the Danish households own a second home (in total, about 200,000 dwellings).

Table 5.1 Housing stock by tenure sector, 1950, 1970, 1990, and 1994, absolute numbers and percentages

1000 dwellings	Owner-occupiers(1)	Non-profit rented sector	Private commercial rental	Unknown	Total
1950	576 (46)	116 (9)	509 (41)	53 (4)	1,254
1970	846 (49)	328 (19)	524 (30)	45 (3)	1,743
1990	1,328 (56)	482 (20)	432 (18)	111 (5)	2,353
1994	1,349 (56)	494 (21)	457 (19)	113 (5)	2,413

(1) Including the cooperative sector.
Source: Boligministeriet, 1994; Van de Ven, 1995, p. 135.

Over the past few years, policy for the non-profit sector has been focused largely on the following key issues:
a) Decentralization. Previously, the state set a quota on the amount of new residential construction that could take place in each municipality. Under the new system, the local authorities can decide for themselves how many new dwellings should be built.
b) Cost control. The maximum allowable cost for standard construction was frozen. Because of the recession in the building trade, which has been going on since 1990, this measure has not had any impact on the quality of new dwellings, at least not yet.
c) Tenant responsibility for the dwelling. There is no income ceiling for the non-profit rented sector. The affluent renters have to be given an incentive to remain in their non-profit rented unit. Therefore, the renters are allowed to adapt their dwelling and invest in it.
d) Social problems. Affluent households tend to move away from certain complexes and neighborhoods. The landlords and the municipality are making a concerted effort to introduce measures to retain these households.
e) The sharp drop in construction. Due to the declining demand, there is no longer a need for large numbers of non-profit rental dwellings. The government has expressed a desire to start subsidizing the other rental sectors in the future, specifically the cooperative and the private rented sector (Van de Ven, 1995, p. 141).

5.2 The institutional structure

The term social rented sector is not entirely applicable to the Danish context. There, this sector is accessible to all income groups. The Danish themselves do not use the term social rented sector (at least not any more) but call it the non-profit rented sector. we Accordingly, we will follow their usage in this chapter.

In Denmark, the non-profit rented sector is of average size, by European standards, comprising about 21 percent of the housing stock. There are roughly 650 non-profit housing associations in Denmark, each of which operates in one and only one municipality. Depending on its size, each municipality will one or more non-profit organizations; the average is two. On average, the associations are fairly small (operating about 1,100 dwellings). They vary widely in terms of their holdings. These housing associations are more or less autonomous private organizations. Many non-profit organizations are allied with one of the organizations that operate at the national or regional level. Those higher-level organizations provide various services for the associations. They keep the books, for instance, help with the planning and administration of new construction, and sometimes provide capital for building or other activities. Most non-profit landlords are members of the umbrella organization Boligskabernes Landsforening (Skifter Andersen, 1994).

Within the non-profit rented sector, we can differentiate between the self-regulating organizations and shareholder organizations. The main difference lies in the number of seats on the board of directors that are reserved for representatives of the local authority. The municipality holds a majority of the seats on the board of these independent or self-regulating organizations (which constitute over half of the all the associations). Any important decisions they make, such as new construction projects or changes in the structure of the organization, require prior approval by the local authority.

In the second type, the shareholder organization, the tenants are shareholders. They own a share, albeit a small one, in the housing stock of the organization. The municipality is not represented on the board. Nonetheless, the local authority has to approve the annual budgets and the books. In this capacity, the municipality can set conditions. For instance, the local authority can insist that rent increases will cover maintenance costs. About 40 percent of the housing associations are of this type. The tenants are members of the association and their right to a dwelling is derived from that membership (Van de Ven, 1995, p. 138).

At the head of a non-profit organization is the board of directors. The majority of the members of the board are elected tenants. In addition, the board consists of representatives of the personnel. In the case of self-regulating organizations, representatives of the local authority are also on the board.

Every non-profit organization is divided into several sections. These are dwellings in a complex or project. Each section has a board that is made up of tenants who have been elected by the members. This increases the influence as well as the commitment of the residents. The relation between tenant and income is strengthened by the fact that income has to cover the operating costs of the complex. The boards constitute the legal basis for the Danish tenant-landlord model. The boards of the sections have authority over how to spend part of the section's funds; the funds may be spent on maintenance or on social activities, for instance. Sometimes, the decisions may imply a large increase in rents. For that eventuality, a minority protection clause has been included. This clause states that if 25 percent of the tenants so desire, a referendum must be held. In addition, the annual general meeting has to approve the budgets and annual reports (Van de Ven, 1995, p. 138).

From time to time, conservative politicians come up with proposals to privatize the non-profit sector even further. To date, proposals along these lines have not been met with enthusiasm. A complicating factor is that the dwellings are not publicly owned. As pointed out earlier, only the self-regulating organizations have representatives of the local authority on their board of directors, and the municipalities have a great deal of influence on these organizations. This is not the case in shareholder organizations.

5.3 Supervision

The task of supervising the organizations is spread over three parties: the local authorities, the personnel, and the tenants. As mentioned in the previous section, the municipality plays a dominant supervisory role. This is because municipal approval is required on all major decisions; for instance, approval would be needed to develop new construction projects or to make significant changes in the organization. Furthermore, the municipality is supposed to approve the annual budgets of the housing associations and review their bookkeeping.

5.4 Subsidies for the non-profit rented sector

Object subsidies and operating subsidies

In Denmark, object subsidies take the form of help with interest payments. These subsidies are linked to two systems of financing: basic financing and financing by way of indexed loans. (For a more detailed description of these financing systems, see Section 5.5 below.) Specific criteria have been developed for the production of non-profit rented dwellings.

Basic financing constitutes seven percent of the total investment costs. The percentage is higher (13 percent, in 1993) in the case of housing for the elderly. The subsidy component lies in the fact that the loans are extended at virtually no interest while repayment of the principal does not occur during the first 50 years. In practice, this amounts to a full subsidy. The loans (subsidies) are provided by local government.

The second form of object subsidy is the system of indexed loans. This system was introduced in 1982 as a way to control the increase in object subsidies. In 1995, financing with an indexed loan covered 91 percent of the investment costs of non-profit dwellings, 96 percent of the dwellings earmarked for youth, and 85 percent of the dwellings intended for the elderly (the latter two figures refer to 1993).

These loans are required for all types of subsidized residential construction. The local authority takes care of the interest payments. The difference between the contract rent, which is established in accordance with legal criteria, and the cost of the indexed loan, which is financed on the capital market, constitutes the government subsidy.

Incidentally, institutional investors who hold shares derived from the indexed loans do not pay tax on income generated by those shares. For this reason, the interest rates on index shares are lower than the rates for nominal shares. For example, the interest on indexed loans was a mere 3.64 percent in 1995. For ordinary loans, the rate was 8.45 percent (OTB survey on financing in the social rented sector, 1996).

The subsidy component is couched in this difference. The contract rent is related only to the conditions for repayment of the loan. Because the loan is indexed, the payments increase annually in nominal terms. In real terms, however, the repayment of the principal remains the same (Papa, 1992, p. 78).

The two kinds of object subsidy described here allowed roughly 35 to 50 percent of the initial costs of a non-profit rented dwelling to be subsidized by the government (European Commission, 1993, p. 96).

Rent subsidy and rent-setting

Denmark has two regimes of rent subsidy. One system is for retired persons, the other is for those who are not retired. The aim of both systems is to ensure a reasonable relation between household income and housing costs. The amount of subsidy depends on the household income, the number of persons in the household, and the size of the dwelling in square meters. Retired persons receive a higher amount of subsidy than non-retired persons (Papa, 1992).

Government expenditure on rent subsidy has been increasing rapidly over the past few years. The government outlay in the period 1990-1993 grew by 33 percent. This increase was the result of a rise in the amounts paid out per household and the increased number of households that are eligible for rent subsidy (Boligministeriet, 1994, p. 15).

Rents in the non-profit sector are based on the historic cost price. The rents have to be in balance with the incomes and outlays at the level of the housing complex. The maintenance costs and the repayment of the loan determine the outlays. In addition, the rent charged per square meter is determined by the unit's geographic location, its design (rents are lower in highrise than in lowrise dwellings, in part reflecting the difference in maximum allowable initial costs), and the individual tenants, who set the amount to be reserved for maintenance. The municipality is responsible for ensuring that these reserves are adequate. If not, the local authority can impose a rent increase, making it possible to build up reserves.

It should be kept in mind that the government does set a legal maximum on the price per square meter. Each quarter, these maximum prices are adjusted to keep pace with wage developments. In this way, it is possible to take the presence of common areas into account. Space for use by all the residents is an amenity that the Danish government wants to promote (Boligministeriet, 1988a, p. 3).

The improvement of dwellings is subsidized in the same way as new residential construction. Since 1982, new renovation projects have been subsidized through the system of interest payments on indexed loans.

5.5 Financing in the non-profit rented sector

The Danish non-profit landlords borrow on the capital market to finance new construction, renovation, and urban renewal activities. According to the respondents who took part in our survey, there is more than adequate financing available for all non-profit organizations.

The financing of new construction in the non-profit rented sector takes place along three lines: a basic financing (seven percent), an indexed loan (91 percent), and a tenant's contribution (two percent). For renovation of the dwelling, the basic financing covers 20 percent of the cost, while the indexed loan covers the other 80 percent. Housing for youth and the elderly has to meet specific criteria. Table 5.2 shows the forms of financing for the three categories of subsidy. The figures for non-profit dwellings are from 1995, while the figures for housing youth and the elderly are from 1993.

Table 5.2 Financing source by subsidy category in Denmark, 1993 and 1995

	Non-profit rented dwellings (1995)	Housing for the elderly	Housing for youth
Indexed loans	91	85	96
Local basic financing	7	13	4
Tenant's contribution	2	2	0
Total	100	100	100

Source: Collignon et al., 1993, p. 102.

The system of basic financing was introduced in 1975 as a way to make the construction of social housing less susceptible to fluctuations on the capital market. At that time, the loans covered 23 percent of the total investment cost. At present, the share of the basic financing for non-profit rented dwellings is a mere four percent. The municipality acts as the lender. The loans are interest-free, and no payments on the principal are required for the first 50 years.

Together with the long-term financing of capital goods, financing the construction of housing is part of a strictly regulated market in Denmark. The legal framework for this financing is formed by the Mortgage Credit Act and the Index-linked Mortgage Lending Act (Boligstyrelsen, 1989, p. 80). This legislation stipulates which organizations are permitted to provide long-term loans on real estate, in which manner the capital for these loans is supposed to be obtained, under which conditions these loans may be extended, and how much guarantee is required.

In Denmark, it is common practice to distinguish between the short-term financing during construction and the long-term financing during the period of residence (that is, the period of operation). Short-term financing is generally offered by banks, especially savings institutions. The long-term financing of dwellings, existing loans (especially indexed loans) on rented dwellings, and renovation is largely arranged through mortgage banks. Denmark has only five institutions that are permitted to offer long-term financing for such purposes. Three of these are active on the home finance market, namely BRFkredit, Kreditforeningen Danmark, and Nykredit. Together with the two other institutions, which are geared to the needs of industry and agriculture, these banks form the Realkreditrådet. This institution functions as a branch organization (Papa, 1992, p. 79).

The five institutions obtain their capital by special bond issues. An important characteristic of such special issues is that the guarantee required on these bonds is specified in real commodities (such as land, buildings, machinery, and so forth). This requirement is set by law (Boligstyrelsen, 1989, p. 80). The value of the good that is financed determines the amount of the mortgage. This differs from common practice in many other countries, where the amount is determined by a guarantee on the person or the organization that takes on the mortgage. The creditworthiness and the income of the person or organization then largely determine the degree to which financing can be obtained. Incidentally, a similar test is common practice in Denmark for short-term financing. This means that the amount of the long-term loan depends on the estimated value of the goods that are to be financed. At the same time, this implies that the loan is inalienable from the good. Since 1990, a few discretionary elements have been built into the system. For instance, mortgage banks are now allowed to arrange a small proportion of the funding in another way besides floating bonds. Furthermore, to a certain extent, some imbalance is allowed between the amounts received by the borrowers and the obligations to the bondholders. This imbalance may not run more than one percent of the organization's reserves, however. In addition, the shareholders have greater security. In the event the mortgage institution should go bankrupt, the claims of mortgage shareholders have priority over the claims of other creditors. The parties who acquire these shares -- mostly life insurance companies and pension funds -- consider them to be identical to government bonds.

As pointed out earlier, the mortgage institutions finance their loans with special bond issues. The law gives the mortgage banks a monopoly on issuance of these special stocks or mortgage bonds. Every time a loan is closed stipulating a nominal interest rate, a life span, and a repayment schedule, the same amount is put up at the same nominal rate of interest, for the same term, and with the same pattern of repayment. By this means, the interest risk is canceled for these organizations. Also these conditions are legally prescribed.

The mortgage bonds are negotiable paper and as such are traded on the Danish stock exchange. The interest margin, which is the difference between the interest that the borrower should pay and the interest that the mortgage bank reimburses to the holder of the mortgage bond, runs between 0.3 and 0.5 percent. Because the bonds are traded on the stock exchange, the issue price is also important. For example, at an issue price of 89.75, when the nominal amount the borrower needs is DK 1,104,000, the mortgage bonds will be issued at a value of DK 1,230,000.

Table 5.3 gives an overview of the market share of various financial institutions in extending long-term loans with commodities as collateral. The table demonstrates the predominant position of the five mortgage banks affiliated with the Realkreditrådet. It should be noted that the share of these institutions declined from 91 percent in 1987 to 84 percent in 1989. This drop reflects a change in credit policy.

As pointed out in Section 5.4, indexed loans have been prescribed for the financing of social rented dwellings since 1982. These indexed loans are also extended by the mortgage institutions that we have just described. Indexed financing was mainly introduced to reduce the initial costs of new dwellings. The interest and repayment of principal are linked to the price index for consumer goods. Twice per year, in January and July, the current debt is adjusted by 75 percent of the rise in the index, beginning a half year after the loan is taken out. The system has a so-called wage index clause. If the rise in the wage index is less steep that the rise in the price index, the current debt is adjusted to that index.

Table 5.3 Registered long-term loans by financing institution, 1987-1989 (percentages)

	1987	1988	1989
Mortgage institutions	91.1	86.1	83.6
Banks	2.4	4.5	6.0
Savings banks	1.7	3.3	4.2
Institutional investors	0.2	0.6	0.9
Other	4.6	5.5	5.3
Total	100.0	100.0	100.0
(million DK)	(92.7)	(95.2)	(89.5)

Source: Realkreditrådet, 1990, p. 38; Papa, 1992, p. 80.

The government takes care of the interest payments on loans to build social housing. As mentioned earlier, the interest on indexed loans was a mere 3.64 percent in 1995. The non-profit landlord only repays the principal. The amount of the annual repayment of principal is calculated in the following way. The first installment is set at 2.4 percent of the original borrowed sum. To determine the next payment, the remaining debt should first be adjusted in accordance with the index. The term of the loan depends on the rate of inflation. The life of the loan is set in the first year on the grounds of the level of inflation. Until 1990, the maximum life of a loan was 35.5 years. Since 1990, the maximum is 50.5 years. When there is no inflation, the term is 35.5 years in the present system. When the inflation is 14.5 percent, the term of the loan is 50.5 years. If the actual development of inflation during the period of operation deviates from the rate of the first year, the loan will either be repaid prematurely or the originally calculated term will be overrun. If a portion of the debt remains after the end of the term that had been set in the first year of the loan, this debt has to be repaid as a lump sum or else must be refinanced (Boligministeriet, 1984; Papa, 1992, pp. 79-85). The respondents to our questionnaire indicated that the term of loans is currently in the range of 40 to 45 years.

In addition to the basic financing and the indexed loans, the Danish system also entails a tenant's contribution. The last two percent of the financing is provided by the tenants themselves in the form of a deposit. That contribution does not apply to housing for youth. No interest is reimbursed for that deposit. The tenant gets this sum back when moving out, if he or she leaves the dwelling in good condition.

As elsewhere, Denmark links the annual demand for financing in the non-profit rented sector to the volume of the new construction program (Table 5.4). Since 1994, the local authorities are allowed to determine the new construction program independently. The State, meanwhile, continues to provide the lion's share of the subsidy on repayment. At some point, the total volume of construction activity that has been planned by the local authorities will exceed a specified level. At that point, the general

Table 5.4 Annual development of new construction in the non-profit rented sector compared with the total number of completions in Denmark, 1980-1995, and projected production, 1996-1997

	Number of completed non-profit dwellings	Number of housing starts	Share of non-profit rented dwellings (%)
1980	6,600	13,800	48
1985	6,600	22,600	29
1986	-	-	-
1987	-	-	-
1988	-	-	-
1989	-	26,000	-
1990	10,600	27,200	39
1991	8,600	20,400	42
1992	5,400	16,400	33
1993	4,800	14,000	34
1994	3,450	-	-
1995	3,034	-	-

Source: Westergard, 1989, p. 7; European Commission, 1994; OTB survey on financing in the social rented sector, 1996.

subsidy, which the government allocates to the local authorities, will be reduced in proportion to the excess number of dwellings (Collignon et al., 1993, p. 33).

The total amount of new housing produced in 1995 was about 3,034 units. Assuming an average initial cost of DK 745,000 (NLG 219,030) per dwelling (which means DK 9,300 per square meter) and an indexed loan of 91 percent, then the total financing demand in Denmark for new construction of non-profit rented dwellings is DK 2,070,705,000 (NLG 608,787,000).

5.6 Risk and guarantees

The Danish government guarantees that portion of the indexed loans in excess of the 65 percent of the value of the loan for new residential construction. The State and the municipality jointly guarantee the remainder. The umbrella organization of non-profit landlords provides a guarantee for the share of financing for renovation that the municipality does not cover. Incidentally, according to the respondents to our questionnaire, less than one percent of the non-profit landlords in Denmark had run into financial problems over the past few years. They also pointed out that a few non-profit landlords have gone bankrupt in recent years; this share is also less than one percent. According to the respondents, the non-profit landlords still see financial management primarily as a bookkeeping task. Only the large landlords have integrated their financial management and risk assessment in the overall management of their organization.

The non-profit housing associations in Denmark are not allowed to undertake any economic activities other than the provision of housing. They are not permitted to turn a profit, nor are they allowed to save. Each section constitutes an economic unit that has to cover its expenditures out of income from rent. The only purpose for which they are expected to build up reserves is for maintenance and improvement. The risk of financial setbacks is thus limited.

Tenants in Denmark's non-profit rented sector are taken seriously in decision-making processes. This is referred to as tenants' democracy. Overall, their say in management affairs has a beneficial effect, since the tenants are drawn into decision-making on all major issues. At the same time, a conflict of interest might arise between tenant and landlord. The reason is that tenants are mainly interested in keeping rents low, less so in long-term upkeep.

This problem has been dealt with in legal terms by setting up a mutual funding organization. The organizations that have to contribute are mostly those with an old dwelling stock. Older non-profit organizations have already paid off their loans and are thus able to build up reserves. This reflects the fact that these landlords are not allowed to lower the rents after their loans have been paid off. Organizations that want to build new dwellings can obtain low-cost loans from this mutual fund. They can also use the loan to finance maintenance activities.

5.7 Opportunities for outside lenders

We may conclude that there are limited opportunities for outside investors to perform in the capacity of lenders to the non-profit rented sector in Denmark. This is due to the fact that the capital market in Denmark is tightly regulated. There is a legal framework defining which organizations are allowed to extend long-term mortgages on real estate. Furthermore, there are laws that spell out how the capital for these loans can be obtained, under which conditions these loans may be arranged, and what kind of guarantee is required. It is possible, however, to buy mortgage bonds from the three accredited mortgage banks. In practice, investors in Denmark equate these shares with government bonds. In this way, the tenants who own shares in the mortgage have priority over other creditors in the event the mortgage bank goes bankrupt. Indirectly, thus, both investors and banks certainly do have good opportunities to invest in the non-profit rented sector. The interest that is reimbursed on these shares is limited, however. That is partly due to the fact that there is no tax on the income that institutional investors derive from the shares based on indexed loans. In that way, the level of interest on indexed shares is lower than that on nominal shares. The low level of risk is the reason why the difference between the interest that the borrower has to pay and the interest that the mortgage bank reimburses to the holder of the mortgage bond is low, in the range of 0.3 to 0.5 percent.

6
GERMANY[1]

J. Smith

6.1 Introduction

The housing sector in Germany differs from that in many other European countries in having a large rental sector and a relatively low level of owner-occupation. Historically and culturally, renting has been the dominant form of housing provision. The nature of the rental market in Germany in terms of its organization and financing makes it very difficult to clearly distinguish between private and social renting (Oxley, 1995, p. 61).

Social housing in Germany is a function of a method of financing housing and not of specific types of landlords. Since 1950 finance and subsidies for the provision of social housing have been available to any registered institution, private individual, company, or institutional investor who agrees to adhere to a number of conditions. These concern rent levels and the income levels of the tenants they accept. There is thus an overlap between "private" and "social" landlords providing social housing.

While difficulties are apparent in defining rental tenure differences, some approximations can be made. Table 1 below illustrates tenure distinctions based on the use of the dwelling not on the type of provider. Some 1.3 million social rented dwellings are actually privately owned (McCrone and Stephens, 1995).

The main incentive that encourages "private" landlords to enter into social housing provision is that they are permitted to make profits. "Social" landlords provided, until 1990, non-profit housing and operated under stricter regulations than private landlords. Since 1990, the regulations concerning non-profit housing have undergone a number of changes. These will be discussed below. Subsidies and loans are available for both rented and owner-occupied social housing. However, the concentration here will be on the social rental sector.

---

[1] Most information and data refer to the former West Germany, unless otherwise stated. Much of the material in this chapter comes from Oxley and Smith (1996).

Table 6.1 Housing stock by tenure

Percentages	1978	1990
Owner-occupied	38	40
Private rented	45	40
Social housing	18	20

Source: McCrone and Stephens, 1995; Oxley and Smith, 1996.

A main feature of the social housing system is that the provisions are temporary in nature. The conditions applicable to social housing apply only until public loans are redeemed. As a result, since the mid-1980s large sections of the social housing stock have been lost to the free sector as these loans are paid off. With only limited new social house building to replace these units, the sector is beginning to experience serious shortages.

6.2 The institutional structure

The overlaps in the provision of social housing in Germany make classification of different landlord organizations difficult. Each landlord does not necessarily provide one specific type of housing. The private landlords who provide social housing are mainly large institutions and private individuals, all of whom make a profit on their investments. This form of social housing provision was undertaken in postwar Germany to encourage increased construction in the sector without putting too great a burden on government finances. However, the profits of these landlords will determine future expansion in this part of the social rented sector. Its growth is therefore tied, more so than in other countries, to both the market and the economy. This can lead to a situation where housing managers, aiming to optimize operating conditions, are necessarily less concerned with ideas of social responsibility towards tenants.

Loans and subsidies are received directly from the government for the construction of dwellings. Private landlords are liable to pay normal company taxes. But the provision of social housing can enable them to take advantage of certain tax concessions. Profits are permitted provided that landlords accept tenants whose incomes are under a specified level, and social rents are charged.

All non-profit housing provided prior to 1990 by social landlords was subject to a Law governing "Housing for the Public Good" (Wohnungsgemeinützigkeitsgesetz). This law decreed that social landlords were exempt from corporate, trade, and capital taxes as a compensation for adhering to the following conditions for supplying social housing:
- a maximum of four percent yield on investment;

- the building and managing of housing was to be a social landlord's sole objective: all other activities were prohibited;
- a commitment that any surpluses above a four percent return would be reinvested in housing;
- rents would be set according to a "social-cost rent principle";
- social landlords would be committed to a continuing building program;
- they would provide for tenants on moderate incomes (within set limits) and accordingly limit the size of the dwellings.

(COFACE, 1989; Power, 1993; Norton and Novy, 1991).

Social landlords that adhere to these regulations are Genossenschaften (cooperative associations) or Wohnungsbaugesellschaften (limited liability housing companies). These are registered with the Gesamtverband der Wohnungswirtschaft (GdW), which is the umbrella organization for non-profit landlords. The GdW acts as a lobby and advice center for the movement, with a regional and federal network.

In 1992 there were 1,827 member organizations in the GdW controlling a total stock of over 3.3 million dwellings. However, not all of these were in the social rented sector. Some of the non-profit organizations have a further role as builders and developers of owner-occupied housing and also manage housing for third parties. These landlords may additionally play a role in providing social housing for profit, so that all of their activities are not bound by the "public good" law.

Cooperative associations make up around two-thirds of the GdW membership (1,174 associations in 1992) but control only about 30 percent of the registered stock; i.e. just over one million dwellings. They are private organizations backed by, for example, churches, trade unions and charities and they have strong local links which influence tenant selection. The cooperative movement is based on collective property and members are owners and tenants at the same time. Tenants are required to pay a proportion of the initial costs of the dwelling and therefore tend to be fairly high-income earners.

Housing companies make up a much smaller part of the GdW membership (622 in 1992) yet they manage a much larger proportion of the social rented stock. They are controlled by municipalities, trade unions, and national employers such as the post office, railways, and churches. A lot of the companies are very small. However, a limited number of them are responsible for large stocks of dwellings. For example, the 50 biggest companies have stocks of approximately 20,000 units each. These companies are usually ones where big-city local authorities or Länder governments have a controlling stake.

During the 1980s total dwelling construction in the social sector fell, as it appeared that the current housing supply was saturating the market. It was said that social housing was no longer needed and that there were many inefficiencies in its provision. These arguments were reinforced when scandal erupted over Neue Heimat, the largest social housing company in Germany, which went bankrupt in the late 1980s.

The crisis had a huge effect on German housing organizations. It gave the government the impetus to change the social housing sector, even though Neue

Heimat was by no means representative of other companies. In 1990 an Act came into effect that repealed the "public good" law. This meant that social housing companies would be allowed to diversify their activities, they would be liable to the same taxes as private landlords and profit-making companies, but they would also receive the same tax privileges (Power, 1993).

It is expected that many cooperatives will voluntarily maintain the conditions of the "public good" law and continue to operate on a non-profit basis. Many organizations have welcomed the changes as they removed many "excessive restrictions" in social housing (COFACE, 1989, p.138). However, there are also fears that the new freedom will lead to increasing rents in the sector, to properties being aimed at higher-income earners to increase profits, and to declining levels of social housing provision. Indeed, the abolition of the "public good" law has been described as the "greatest wrong decision since the war" (German Tenant Association, Director H. Schlich in Frankfurter Rundschau, 21.1.89, quoted in Norton and Novy, 1991, p. 32).

6.3 Supervision

The relationships between the government and the housing bodies responsible for the construction and improvement of social rented dwellings are concerned mainly with financial arrangements. The federal government determines the amount of subsidy to be allocated to the social housing program each year. The Länder governments are obliged to allocate an amount to social housing equal to that which the central government is allocating to their Land. They are responsible for awarding social housing subsidies and loans resulting from the social housing program together with any they wish to grant from their own budgets (via, for example, the Third Way subsidy path).

More recently, however, the Länder have had to make increasing contributions to the social housing programs over and above their "legal" requirements. This is largely due to pressures on the housing market and the limits of the social housing finance system. It meant that in 1992, out of DM 20 billion in direct subsidies to social housing, DM 16.3 billion (82 percent) came from the Länder and DM 3.7 billion (18 percent) from the federal government (UNFOHLM, 1994).

The Länder decide how funds are allocated to each of the three Förderungswege. The framework for subsidizing social housing construction (outlined in more detail below) represents the broad regulatory structure at the federal level. It is important to note, however, that a large degree of diversity in the channeling of social housing finance and the conditions of loans and subsidies exists between the Länder who have control at this level. The Länder make decisions concerning the number of dwellings to be built over the year and whether these are to be for rent or sale. The Länder also set the criteria for the quality of the dwellings.

The municipalities, in turn, take responsibility for urban planning matters. They issue construction permits, allocate social dwellings, and provide land on which to build social housing.

There has been some concern over the apparent low level of monitoring of social housing landlords, especially following the Neue Heimat incident described above. Some discussions have taken place as to possibilities for supervision. Yet there are significant difficulties because of the large variety of different types of landlords providing social housing. Some degree of monitoring can be undertaken with those landlords registered with the social housing umbrella organization, the GdW. However, as more and more non-profit landlords are repealing their "public good" status, the issue of supervision and monitoring is becoming increasingly problematic.

6.4 Subsidies for the social rented sector

Construction of social rented dwellings

There are three main subsidy paths (Förderungswege) provided by the central and Länder governments for the construction of social housing. Their principal aim is to reduce the tenants' rents to below the "cost rent." The size of the loan will therefore be different for each development project.

The first subsidy path (Erster Förderungsweg) is for the construction of publicly assisted social housing reserved for specific segments of the population. This subsidy is awarded on the condition that minimum quality standards are met in building. A dwelling must also be below a maximum quality standard to be allocated to a social tenant. Tenants must have incomes under a set ceiling.

The second subsidy path (Zweiter Förderungsweg) leads to the construction of dwellings which are slightly above the level of those constructed under the First Way. They are allocated to households whose incomes are up to 40 percent above the social income limit. They will have a higher rent attached to them. Therefore, these units are intended for tenants who have higher incomes but cannot afford to rent in the free private sector.

Some Länder also offer a Third Way (Dritte Förderungsweg). This was introduced in 1986 so that Länder can grant further (usually short-term) subsidies for social housing construction with more flexible arrangements concerning rent-setting and allocation. The conditions are arranged between the Länder and the "builder" when the subsidy is awarded (Hallett, 1993, p. 126).

The actual financial instruments used are set out below.
There are three forms of aid that are used for the Erster and Zweiter Förderungswege:

i, Capital subsidy in the form of a low-interest loan, which will partially finance the construction of a dwelling;

ii, Operating costs subsidy, usually paid over a 15-year period with the subsidy decreasing each year. The size of the original subsidy depends on the floor space of the dwelling;

iii, Operating cost loans to partially cover capital expenditure. The amount of the loan will depend on floor space. Loans are given for 15 years. Again, the amount paid in the first year is reduced annually. Repayments of 2 percent per year begin from the sixteenth year. Interest at 6 percent on the unrepaid part of the loan must also be paid from the sixteenth year. When loans have been repaid, usually over 30 years, the dwellings revert to the free rental sector with a market rent.

Generally, institutions constructing social rented dwellings must finance at least 15 percent of the building costs themselves. As well as subsidized loans from the Länder, loans can be taken up from the capital market. These are loans on an annuity basis with a term of 30 years (Papa, 1992, p. 61). If an operating cost subsidy has been allocated, subsidies may also be given in the form of sureties for mortgages which are obtained at market rates (Hubert, 1992).

From 1977, subsidies to encourage the improvement of rented dwellings took two forms: low-interest loans and operating subsidies. These were financed jointly by the federal and Länder governments and were implemented through the municipalities. Schemes were targeted at older urban areas and on energy-saving projects (Tomann, 1990).

From 1985, the federal government withdrew from the direct financing of social housing as, for reasons discussed earlier, the necessity for social house building was not seen as being so great. This left the responsibility for financing all new social housing developments entirely to the Länder and municipalities. That situation led to the development of the Dritte Förderungsweg. Even so, the late 1980s saw a dramatic downturn in the construction of new social dwellings. It was only from 1989 that the federal government again started to grant direct subsidies for new building. This action was brought on largely by reunification. It was also influenced by the increasing need for housing and the shortfall of "one million dwellings" discovered after the 1987 census (Eekhoff, 1989).

The federal government has set out a program for its budget allocations to social housing up to 1997. These have been increased considerably since the late 1980s. In 1988, federal funds for the social housing program stood at DM 0.45 billion and DM 1.05 billion in 1989. However, between 1990 and 1997, it is estimated that funds will average out at approximately DM 3 billion per annum, including subsidies for the new Länder.

Rent subsidies and rent-setting policy
A scale of social rent levels is set annually by the Länder. These are the rents that tenants in social dwellings actually pay. For individual landlords to arrive at this social rent, they must initially make a calculation of cost rents, which will then be adjusted down to the social rent through negotiation of different subsidies. (The description of the system of social-cost rent calculations relies heavily on Hubert, 1993).

The cost rent must be calculated for each individual project. It is based on an estimation of construction costs, land costs, and interest on loans where appropriate throughout the construction period. From all of these items, a "cost rent" is arrived at. The difference between the cost rent and the social rent set by the Länder is made up by a subsidy payment through one of the subsidy paths. The investor gets a return equivalent to the cost rent (social rent plus subsidy). The cost rent is binding until public loans or subsidies are fully repaid and the dwellings revert to the free rental sector.

Increases in rent are dealt with differently, depending on the type of financing and subsidy awarded. The different systems of rent increases caused problems to tenants, as landlords can pass on increased costs. Social rents have been rising at increasing rates. Higher rents have not been accompanied by increases in incomes to the degrees that were anticipated in the methods of rent calculation. Thus, rising rents have been an increasing burden on tenants. A substantial difference has grown between rents of dwellings financed by public loans and those financed by expenditure subsidies.

According to general Tenure Law, 11 percent of all improvement costs can be passed on in higher rents. This led many landlords to carry out extensive improvements purely so that they could charge an increased rent. This means that many tenants experienced great hardship in meeting higher rental demands. Changes are being made to the system so that the cost rents are not being set so high.

Income is the main criterion for determining whether a household is in need of a social dwelling. Once an individual has tenancy, there are no further reviews of household income. This has led to considerable problems as tenants' incomes rise above the qualifying level, and they are still able to stay in the dwelling.

There was much debate about how to address this problem. With growing need for social housing, it seemed that the sector was not targeted to those in most need, and that the rate at which new requirements were being met from the existing stock was very low. In response to this situation, the Bundestag introduced a law at the end of 1981 which entitled the Länder to levy an additional tax on certain households. This tax, the Fehlbelegungsabgabe, must be paid by tenants if their incomes rise to 20 percent above the set limit. The setting of the limits and the operation of the system vary between the Länder. The revenue received from this tax is put back into new social housing construction (Hills *et al.*, 1990, p. 155).

Even after some years of operation, the additional tax does not seem to have been very effective at providing an incentive for high-income tenants to move on. Problems of allocation and access are therefore continuing.

The Wohngeld housing allowance system was introduced in Germany in 1965. The system stipulated that payment for adequate accommodation should not exceed 15 to 25 percent (or up to 30 percent for individuals) of the total spending of the household. The payments are always directed to the tenant, never the landlord. The main principle of the system is that the payment reduces rents and housing costs and is therefore not treated as a general income supplement. The actual amounts of payments are calculated according to an extensive set of tables. If a household is receiving social benefits, all of its housing costs can be covered and rents can be subsidized 100 percent at the margin.

A maximum income limit exists for Wohngeld, which will increase as the number of earners in a household increases. Housing allowances are subject to a maximum rent level. This is adjusted every few years to take account of changing incomes and rents. Between 1965 and 1991, nine adjustments to this limit occurred (Bundesministerium, 1992). The system is inherently problematic because, in the periods between adjustments, rents and incomes will be rising but the limits for Wohngeld qualification will remain the same. This leads to households gradually "outgrowing" the system in these periods, possibly facing difficulties in meeting rents, and then re-qualifying when the limit is adjusted.

About 10 percent of all tenants receive housing allowances. Various additional housing allowances have been introduced in many Länder to help households experiencing difficulties due to the Wohngeld system. They only apply in the social sector. These schemes operate in a similar way to housing allowances and take a number of different forms: Härteausgleich - a hardship compensation; Mietgarantie - a rent guarantee; or Mietausgleich - a rent compensation.

There is significant debate in Germany surrounding the reform of subsidy to social housing and method of calculating rents because of some of the problems that have been identified here. A particular concern is that subsidized housing must be geared more to the income of the tenant rather than to covering construction costs. Current subsidy schemes are seen as somewhat inflexible. Reform suggestions include readjusting the balance of aid between investment and consumption of housing to improve allocation of subsidies. This is focused to some extent on reform of the rent subsidy (UNFOHLM, 1994). In addition, discussions are taking place as to ways of reducing overall construction costs in social housing, which are unusually high compared to other European countries. There is a fairly widespread consensus on the need for change within Germany, although the means by which it is applied continue to be debated.

6.5 Financing in the social housing sector

Finance for constructing social dwellings comes from a number of sources. As described above, a number of financial instruments are available from the federal and Länder governments which partially cover financing. In addition, investors in social housing construction are required to provide some percentage of construction costs themselves and may also utilize capital market loans.

The divisions between these different sources of finance is not set out at a national level. It can vary between the Länder, between cities, and may in practice be different for each development. It will clearly depend on the form of subsidy being taken up and the level of funds the investor is contributing. Most developments are therefore made up of mixed funding from a number of sources. Separate contracts, between the investor and the state, are made for each development. The contracts stipulate financing and subsidy arrangements and determine cost-rent levels, as described previously. There is thus a strong relationship between the allocation of subsidies and the construction costs of a development (Hubert, 1992, p. 7).

Three basic elements make up social housing construction finance. The first one is the investor's own capital and assets. For most institutional investors, this must be a minimum of 15 percent of construction costs. On this 15 percent equity, investors can receive a return of 4 percent; for any equity above 15 percent, they may receive a 6.5 percent return. Also counting as investors assets are direct payments to individuals which may take the form of loans and subsidies from employers for housing, financial compensation for losses in World War II, tenant loans etc.

The second element comprises state loans and subsidies. These are channeled through the Förderungswege described above, with additional funding also being allocated by municipalities to specific cases to target groups. The amount of loan or subsidy provided and the interest rate attached to it vary according to factors such as dwelling size and location and which other financial instruments are included in the "contract." State-subsidized loans may either be interest-free or low-interest public loans or loans from the capital market subsidized by a reduced rate of interest.

Finally, investors in social housing construction may also take up finance from the capital market. These are likely to make up a smaller proportion of overall funding and have a higher rate of interest. Interest rates on a public loan are usually around 1-2 percent but can increase to 6 or 7 percent on a private loan (DIW, 1996; BLR, 1996). The relaxation of controls in the capital market had a positive effect for investors. Mortgage interest rates were reduced during the early 1990s, thus improving incentives for investing in housebuilding (GdW, 1993, p. 34).

The main sources for private capital finance for social housing are mortgage bond institutions, savings banks, private and social insurance companies, housing savings banks, and other money lenders. Where capital finance is subsidized, this may be in the form of lower interest rates or security on interest and repayments. Both are aimed at reducing the rents and charges attached to social dwellings.

For individual developments, the balance between these three types of finance can vary considerably. For example, while state-subsidized finance averages around 20 percent of construction costs, for some developments the state may be subsidizing 40-50 percent of the costs. This may be the case, for example, in deprived areas and for special target groups.

On a national scale (former West Germany), of all finance for social housing in 1994 17.5 percent came from public budgets, 49.2 percent came from the capital market, and 33.3 percent came from investors' assets and other sources. Over the past five years, there has been a slight increase in funding from the capital market and a decrease in that from public budgets. Overall financing has increased, however, from DM 23.2 billion in 1990 to DM 34 billion in 1994.

These proportions are slightly different in the former East German Länder, where, in 1994, 10 percent of the finance for social housing programs came from public funds, 59 percent from the capital market, and 31 percent from investors' assets, totalling DM 17 billion in 1994 (this compares with a total of just DM 0.9 billion in 1991) (Statistisches Bundesamt, 1990, 1991, 1994).

Although an increasing proportion of finance for social housing construction in Germany is coming from the capital market, this is not seen as particularly problematic (in the same way as it is in the UK, for instance). The reason is that much of this capital finance is subsidized and secured by the state (see further discussion in Section 6.6). The specific details of the loans tend to vary across the subsidy paths and among different lending institutions. However, loans are generally extended on 30-year repayment schedules with interest rates fixed according to the proportion of

Table 6.2 Social housing construction, Germany*

	Social housing construction	Total housing construction	Social construction as % of total construction
1980	97175	388904	25
1985	68952	312053	22
1988	38886	208621	19
1989	65153	238617	27
1990	90704	256488	35
1991	93973	314508	30
1992	108474	374606	29
1994	162021	n.a.	n.a.

* Data after 1990 represent unified Germany
Source: Statistisches Bundesamt, 1990, 1991, 1994.

different funding sources, types and location of dwellings, and the length of the lending period.

As a result of significant increases in financing (and government subsidies) available to social housing construction since the late 1980s, social housing completions increased from 90,704 in 1990 to 162,021 in 1994 (figures for both "old" and "new" Bundesländer) (Statistisches Bundesamt, 1994). The trends in social housing construction since 1980 are reflected in Table 6.2.

This table shows the decline in social housing construction at the end of the 1980s. Completions fell to a low of 38,886 social dwellings in 1988, as government subsidies were withdrawn. The significant increase in social housing construction to around 30 percent of all housing production in the mid-1990s is related to the reunification of Germany, the re-introduction of government subsidizes, and the wider availability of capital, as discussed above.

6.6 Risk and guarantees in the social rented sector

The series of contractual arrangements that surround the financing of social housing developments means that the government takes on a significant amount of risk and also plays a role as guarantor. Risk does vary, however, with the types of subsidy being provided by the state. If the subsidies are in the form of current allowances the state will usually insure the second mortgage. But if the state provides a public loan, a second loan from the capital market will have a higher interest rate, for which the bank bears the risk (Hubert, 1992, p. 14). However, because the whole package of financing is arranged to cover construction costs and determines cost-rent levels, and because subsidy is calculated taking into account the cost of all finance, there is a form of state guarantee effectively written into most social housing construction contracts. The Förderungsanstalten of the Länder can also operate as a guarantee for social housing organizations who borrow from the private capital market.

The nature of the financing system has been seen to be extremely generous to investors. There have been criticisms that investors can "profiteer" from social housing programs (Hubert, 1992, p. 5) which has led to calls for a reform of the system. It has also been noted that, "they (social housing programmes) are expensive, providing housing for below market prices and shifting investment risks largely to public budgets" (Tomann, 1994, p. 17). Tomann goes on to say that the state bears too much of the market risk on capital, which should be shifted instead to investors and their creditors (Tomann, 1994, p. 18), and calls for the design of new financial instruments for housing. Reforms in social housing finance and subsidization continue to be debated in Germany, as noted in Section 6.4 above.

6.7 Social housing in the new Bundesländer

Social housing, or at least housing controlled by the state, makes up nearly half of the new Bundesländer housing stock. In 1992, this amounted to 3,370,000 social units out of a stock of nearly seven million dwellings. This has led to a doubling of the amount of social housing in the united Germany.

Public housing was previously managed by state-run and cooperative administrations. The administrations would either own or act as trustees for the dwelling stock. The legal entities responsible for the administration of the state-owned stocks were state-run companies such as VEB Kommunale Wohnungsverwaltung (KWV) and VEB Gebäudewirtschaft (GW). The owners of cooperative housing stocks were workers housing cooperatives (AWG) and non-profit housing cooperatives (GWG).

Financing for these types of housing was provided almost completely by the state, due to the provision of housing being seen as a "social task." Housing construction was financed by state low-interest loans to housing administrations, cooperatives, and to a lesser extent, to individuals for owner-occupation. The loans usually ran for a period of 41 years with interest set at a rate of 4 percent. Loans for the construction of owner-occupied dwellings could, in part, be interest-free. The repayments were worked out so that the monthly financial commitment never exceeded the equivalent of the monthly rent to be paid by the tenants in state-owned flats.

Rents in state dwellings were set and controlled by the government. However, costs of financing and construction were rarely taken into account when determining rent levels. Rents were set according to the circumstances of each household: number of adults and children, age, health, and income. The rents on these dwellings bore little resemblance to costs and were set at very low levels.

Reunification has resulted in the ownership of housing being reorganized to fit into the models of the old Bundesländer. For social housing this has meant changing the state housing administrations into non-profit housing associations/cooperatives, joint stock companies or public limited companies. Many of these organizations have taken up membership of the Gesamtverband der Wohnungswirtschaft (GdW).

The subsidization and financing for social housing programs broadly follows that which is in operation in the former West Germany. Most subsidies are therefore transferred through the three subsidy paths described above. In addition there are significant funds being channelled to housing and urban renewal. City renewal is a central concern which includes the improvement and modernization of large numbers of dwellings, inner-city building and development as well as special projects such as ecological renewal. Much of this work is being financed through tax reductions and subsidized building loans. There is, however, an emphasis on encouraging private finance to contribute to the renewal programs. Most of the improvement and modernization work is being subsidized through interest subsidies and current expenditure subsidies (Bundesministerium, 1993, 1994).

The changeover will be a very gradual process, complicated by the accumulated debts of the GDR housing administrations pre-1989. These debts to state owned credit institutions amounted to DM 36 billion in 1991. Discussions are continuing about how to deal with the problem. The president of the GdW, Jürgen Steinert, is proposing that these state owned dwellings should be controlled by non-profit companies along the lines of those previously operating in the former West Germany, and that the federal government should write off the debts so that housing costs in the country would be moderated, and more money could be channelled into new investment in subsidized housing.

The claims on land and property from outside of the new Bundesländern have also caused many problems. Vast quantities of land and housing have been thrown into effective 'limbo' while ownership's are being determined. At the end of 1991 about 9 per cent of the total housing stock was caught up in restitution claims from third parties or had doubtful property ownership's (GdW, 1992). Of the 3.37 million dwellings in GdW membership, 18 per cent had claims of restitution. Most of these were in the housing companies rather than co-operatives. By the end of 1992, only 83,560 dwellings(14 per cent of all claims) had been returned to their rightful owners. This left 15.5 per cent (522,000 dwellings) of the whole stock with uncertain ownership. This is blocking further investment in these dwellings (GdW, 1993). In the social housing stock there is also a problem of over 90,000 empty dwellings, which need to be made fit to live in. Many of these dwellings can be brought back into use, once repairs have been made.

6.8 Opportunities for outside lenders

It has been reported that there is no lack of finance for potential investors in German social housing construction (DIW, 1996; BLR, 1996). Under the current subsidy and finance arrangements, it seems unlikely that foreign investors would enter into German social housing. However, if changes are made to the current system, there is a potential for new opportunities to arise, particularly in respect to the profits allowed on investors' own capital.

While a number of recent changes have been made to the system of social housing in Germany, considerable problems still remain in the sector. These include:

i, an increasing pressure on waiting lists from immigrants from Eastern Europe, and also movement within Germany since reunification;

ii, increased demand for social dwellings due to increasing household formation;

iii, problems of "under-occupation" of social dwellings as households become smaller but remain in the dwellings of the same size;

iv, access to the social housing stock, difficulties being experienced by "problem households" as landlords become more and more selective;

v, the question of whether social landlords are really fulfilling their "social" obligation. This has been brought even more into question as non-profit status is ended for many organizations;

vi, financing and subsidy system for the social housing program and its overall efficiency.

These issues continue to be debated. A number of questions need to be addressed. Should high-income earners be allowed to remain in the social dwelling stock? Should new immigrants who have never paid into the social welfare system be entitled to receive social housing? There are discussions about how the Fehlbelegungsabgabe might be changed, to increase more proportionately with income.

However, a principal concern is still the need to build more social dwellings. Increasing construction in this sector is now a major policy issue, even more so following the changes in the non-profit status of landlords in 1990 and the reduction of the stock as social loans are repaid. It is a topic fraught with political sensitivity in terms of responsibility between the federal and Länder governments.

7
FRANCE

P.J. Boelhouwer

7.1 Introduction

In contrast to the situation in most other countries of Western Europe, the French government (that is, Paris) has a major influence on policy at the regional and local level. Of course, each administrative level has its own range of authority. Nevertheless, the national government carries out strict supervision of those levels; the official in charge of oversight is the préfet. As in most West European countries, over half of all households in France are homeowners. For decades, the main thrust of French housing policy has been the promotion of owner-occupancy. Despite this government aim, the social rented sector has a strong presence in France, accounting for 17 percent of the country's housing stock. French rental housing is usually classified in the following four sectors (see also Table 7.1):
1. social rented dwellings, called HLM dwellings (Habitations à Loyers Modérés, dwellings with moderate rents);
2. other social rented dwellings (Sociétés d'Économie Mixte (SEM);
3. dwellings that fall under the Rent Act of 1948: the regulated private rented sector;
4. the unregulated private rented sector.

The first two categories comprise the social rented sector. Dwellings in that sector are built with the help of government loans on which the interest is subsidized, called Prêts Locatifs Aidés (PLA). The last two categories comprise the private rented sector.

At present, HLM landlords are faced with a paradox. While providing inexpensive accommodation for low-income groups, they also have to retain the more affluent households as tenants (Van de Ven, 1995, p. 93). The reason to cater to higher-income tenants is that the HLMs have to remain financially sound. In order to keep the financially stronger households, the HLM organizations want to set a limit on the concentration of minorities and other deprived groups, especially in the unpopular highrise complexes. In this context, a past mayor of Grenoble, Mr. Dauge, predicted back in 1991 that unless a new policy is put into place, the social rented sector will become less and less popular and will house more and more poor households. Investment alone will not be sufficient to resolve the social and racial problems (Power, 1993, p. 83).

Table 7.1 Distribution of French households by tenure, 1973, 1988, 1992 (percentages)

	1973	1988	1992
Owner-occupiers	46	54	56
Rented sector, unfurnished, of which:			
- Social:			
HLM	11	15	15
not HLM	- (1)	2	2
- Private:			
Act of 1948	7	2	2
Other	23	17	19
Other (2)	14	9	6
Total x 1000	17,124	21,256	22,131

(1) No separate data available.
(2) Including subletting, rental of furnished dwellings, and dwellings not to be lived in.
Source: INSEE Enquêtes Logement 1988, 1992; Van de Ven, 1995, p. 78.

7.2 The institutional structure

France's social rented sector has a fairly complex institutional structure. As mentioned above, the social rented dwellings are known as HLM dwellings. In 1992, there were roughly 1,000 HLM housing associations. Those organizations have built 4.6 million dwellings. Of this total, about 3.3 million were built as social rented dwellings and 1.3 million were built as owner-occupier dwellings in the social sector (Oxley and Smith, 1996, p. 85). On average, a landlord will own about 4,600 units (Van Harten, 1990; Emms, 1990). Between 65 and 70 percent of the HLM dwellings are located in the grands ensembles, massive highrise complexes that were built in urban extension areas from the 1950s through the 1970s.

The two main segments of the HLM holdings are Offices Publics d'HLM (OPHLM) and Sociétés Anonymes d'HLM (SAHLM). The distinction between the two organizations is primarily legal. The OPHLM is anchored in public law and the SAHLM in private law. In 1993, there were 296 OPHLMs in France (including the OPACs; see below) and 360 SAHLMs (European Commission, 1993; Emms, 1990). The HLMs also have a national umbrella organization, the UNFOHLM (Union Nationale des Fédération d'Organismes de Habitations à Loyer Modéré).

The OPHLM associations may be seen as purely non-profit organizations that are dedicated to the construction and management of inexpensive rental dwellings. On a more modest scale, they also carry out renovation projects and are involved in other urban development projects. The average holding of an OPHLM association is about 6,000 dwellings.

Besides the public OPHLMs, there are also public OPACs (Offices Publics d'Aménagement et de Construction). These organizations were established in 1973 to renovate existing social rented dwellings and build new ones. Sometimes, they took over the holdings of the local HLM landlords (Power, 1993). According to Emms (1990), the main difference between OPHLMs and OPACs lies in the OPACs' greater degree of independence from the government. This independence is expressed in the composition of the board of directors. It includes fewer representatives of the government and more of economic, social, and cultural interest groups. With an average holding of 17,000 dwellings, the OPACs are much larger that the OPHLM associations. Their package of activities is also much more extensive. For instance, they are able to purchase land and develop housing on it (Oxley and Smith, 1996, p. 85).

The SAHLM associations are private organizations that are allowed to make a limited amount of profit. They are usually sponsored by private businesses, but they may also be sponsored by public companies or local authorities. In this way, the organizations try to make sure they can provide housing for their employees (Van Harten, 1990). The SAHLMs are also involved in the construction of subsidized owner-occupancy dwellings for lower-income groups. They have built up a stock of over a million social owner-occupied dwellings (Boelhouwer and Van der Heijden, 1992). Since the 1977 reform of social housing, the SAHLM associations have become the main producers of housing in the social sector. In 1991, 58 percent of all housing starts in the social sector consisted of SAHLM dwellings, while the public branch of the HLM (the OPHLMs and the OPACs) accounted for 42 percent of the starts in social housing (Oxley and Smith, 1996, p. 85).

The Sociétés Co-opératives de HLM and the Sociétés de Crédit Immobilier (SACI) are two smaller non-profit landlords. Their role is less significant than that of the associations discussed above. This is clear from the figures: in the early 1990s, these two associations were responsible for roughly 3.5 percent of the new construction under HLM (Oxley and Smith, 1996; Boelhouwer and Van der Heijden, 1992). The main task of the SACI is to provide both subsidized and unsubsidized loans to homeowners. The organization falls under the Bank Act of 1984, which provides guidelines for financial institutions.

The French social rented sector is not entirely comparable with the Dutch social rented sector. Up to 30 percent of the HLM dwellings can be reserved for employees of specified companies. According to the so-called one percent rule, certain companies with over ten employees have that right. Firms in this category have to invest about 0.7 percent (previously one percent) of the payroll in housing (Van Harten, 1990).

Social rented dwellings are also built and operated by Sociétés d'Économie Mixte (SEMs). Oxley and Smith (1996) report that the SEMs control about ten percent of the social rented housing stock. These are private organizations. For the most part, these joint ventures are privately financed, although the government also makes a contribution. The target group of their efforts consists of households who are unable to enter the private rented sector but whose income is too high for the social rented sector (Emms, 1990).

7.3 Supervision

Lower levels of government (municipalities and departements) sponsor and supervise the OPHLMs. Representatives of the government generally have a majority in the Conseil d'Administration (Van Harten, 1990). The ultimate responsibility for supervision of the HLM associations lies with the préfet, however. Since the Second World War, the government has developed numerous criteria and guidelines that have had the effect of restricting the associations' room to maneuver. However, most influence is exerted through subsidies; this is also the general pattern in the rest of Europe, with the possible exception of the Netherlands.

Financial oversight is performed by a particular financial institution (Caisse des Dépôts et Consignations, CDC), which makes the subsidized loans available. In doing so, the CDC has the right to review the management of the HLM association. If the findings are negative, the CDC can even deny a loan application.

7.4 Subsidies for the social rented sector

Object subsidies and operating subsidies

Since 1977, new residential construction by HLM associations has been subsidized by way of loans with an interest subsidy, called Prêts Locatifs Aidés (PLA). There are two variants in the PLA program. The PLA/CDC loans are intended for the social rented dwellings that are built by the HLM associations. The PLA/I loans (or integration-promoting inexpensive loans for rental dwellings) are intended for the construction or renovation of rental units for families who would otherwise not be able to find an affordable dwelling (Collignon et al., 1993, p. 14).

Both variants may be applied to either new construction or the purchase and renovation of existing dwellings. The latter option is becoming less popular, however, because of the high expense. The HLMs build both rental and owner-occupancy dwellings. Builders and operators of only rental dwellings are not allowed to make a profit. The HLMs that are devoted to the construction of owner-occupancy dwellings are permitted to make a limited amount of profit. They account for roughly two-thirds of the HLM production.

In 1993, the French government started a new real estate investment program for the social rented sector. The main aims of this program are to create jobs, to bolster confidence in investment, and to reduce vacancy (CECODHAS, 1994, p. 19). Besides building 190,000 social rented dwellings (in 1993 and 1994), the plan also envisions the construction of 110,000 social owner-occupancy dwellings and the rehabilitation of 200,000 social rented dwellings.

Under the above-mentioned program of object subsidies, about 66 percent of the initial costs of building a social rented dwelling were subsidized by the government in 1993 with a PLA loan (European Commission, 1993, p. 96).

In addition to the subsidies on new residential construction, the French government also subsidizes the upkeep of dwellings. For this purpose, the government does not provide

interest subsidies. Instead, it offers object subsidies in the form of lump-sum contributions. In the social rented sector, two forms of subsidy may be distinguished:
- subsidies of the ANAH (Agence Nationale pour l'Amélioration de l'Habitat);
- the PALULOS lump-sum contribution (Prime à l'Amélioration des Logement à Usage Locatif et à Occupation Sociale).

The ANAH subsidies are the oldest form of subsidized housing improvement. The ANAH is an organization dedicated to the improvement of rental dwellings. The ANAH only extends subsidies for the renovation of rental units, specifically in the private sector, that were built before 1948. Some conditions are posed on the extension of subsidy. One is that the dwelling has to be rented out for at least ten years after the renovation. Another is that the rent cannot be higher than a specified level. The subsidy consists of standard amounts for specified activities. In this way, the subsidy covers between 30 and 40 percent of the allowable costs, on average. The maximum contribution would normally run up to 50 percent of the costs. But under special building programs, it might run up to 80 percent of the allowable costs (Heugas-Darraspen, 1985, p. 81).

PALULOS is a lump-sum contribution to cover the improvement of social rented dwellings built before 1968. The landlord is supposed to belong to a specified group of organizations, mainly non-profit housing associations. The HLMs fall into this group (Heugas-Darraspen, 1985, p. 83). The contribution can be as high as 20 percent of the renovation costs. For sound and heat insulation, the coverage may be as high as 30-40 percent of the costs (Marchal, 1989).

In addition, the PLA loans are also intended to finance the acquisition of existing dwellings more than 20 years old for the purpose of renovation (Papa, 1992, p. 113).

Another important form of subsidy is provided by the municipality. The local authority can make building sites available to HLM associations. Furthermore, the municipality can grant subsidies when a building site is purchased in an area where the price of land is higher than the reference price. Subsidies of this kind are provided partly by the mutual fund and partly by local government.

Rent subsidy and rent-setting
There are three types of subject subsidies in France. The main one is the individual subsidy, Aide Personnalisée au Logement (APL). Another one is the Allocation de Logement à caractère Social (ALS). Both of these subsidies take the household income into account. But they use different tables to calculate the amounts.

The Aide Personnalisée au Logement (APL) was introduced in 1977. It was intended to gradually replace the object subsidies (Heugas-Darraspen, 1985). The APL applies to renters and to owner-occupiers (half of the outlays for APL go to homeowners). The subsidy is paid from a fund that is fed by the state (Papa, 1992, p. 111).

Not everyone is eligible for an APL subsidy. The program is tied to certain dwellings. Only residents of particular dwellings that were built after 1977 are eligible.

In the rental sector, these are the tenants of social rented dwellings (HLMs) that were built after 1977 and the tenants of dwellings for which the landlord has signed a contract with the state. That agreement, known as the Secteur Conventionné (Heugas-Darraspen, 1985, pp. 58-59), establishes how the state will provide financial support through subsidized loans and the APL program. The agreement also stipulates which quality requirements the dwellings must meet and which income criteria the tenants must meet (Boucher, 1988, p. 313). The amount of the APL depends on the rent level, the size of the household, the household income, and the geographic location of the dwelling. The APL is paid directly to the landlord, who subsequently sets the rent on the basis of the household composition. (For an extensive description of the APL, see Papa, 1992, p. 111.)

The ALF and the ALS are not financed by the Ministry of Housing. The Allocation de Logement à caractère Familial (ALF) is financed by a national fund for subsidies to families. That fund is built up from the contributions of employees (Marchal, 1989). The ALF program traditionally caters to families, but the eligibility rules have been extended to include unmarried persons with children, households taking care of a relative, and young couples (married for less than five years). In 1991, more than one million households received a subsidy under the ALF program, including 800,000 renters. In total, they received 12.4 billion francs (Fribourg, 1994).

The Allocation de Logement à caractère Social (ALS) is part of the system of social benefits. These are paid out of the revenues from social security premiums. The ALS is granted to the elderly, people with a work disability, the unemployed, the youth, the handicapped, and other special groups. The subsidy may be considered as a form of social benefit for persons who are unable to pay their housing costs on their own accord. The regulation dates back to 1971. In 1991, over one million households received an ALS subsidy, amounting to a total of 10.3 billion francs (Fribourg, 1994; Papa, 1992).

The French government controls rents in the social rented sector. The rules reflect the way in which the dwellings are financed. There is a difference between the rules for raising rents under a new rent contract and under an existing one. In principle, rents are based on actual costs.

The legal regulations that apply to HLM rents give the associations the right to raise the rent by up to ten percent per half year. However, they are not allowed to exceed the corrected maximum rent per square meter. That maximum or ceiling is set each year by the Minister of Housing (Fribourg, 1994). The rent was increased by 3.4 percent in 1988, by 2.2 percent in 1989, by 2.5 percent in 1990, and by 2.8 percent in 1991 and 1992 (Fribourg, 1994).

The rent of social rented dwellings that were financed before 1977 is based on the (corrected) floor space. The price per square meter is shown in a table (fourchette) for diverse types of dwelling and years of construction. Rents are expressed in terms of a minimum and a maximum amount, which are determined annually. Each year, the table is adjusted to reflect to construction cost index. These tables also apply to new rent contracts (Wiktorin, 1992). And each year, the government formulates guidelines for rent increases in the social rented sector. Those guidelines are based on the expected rate of inflation for the next year.

Tenants in the social rented sector whose income exceeds a specified maximum are supposed to pay more rent. The maximum is intended to indicate the ceiling for housing allocation. The amount of extra rent to be paid depends on how high the income is, on the contract rent, and on the number and age of members of the household (Wiktorin, 1992, p. 43). In practice, few landlords actually charge their tenants this extra rent (Van de Ven, 1995, p. 91).

7.5 Financing in the social rented sector

The loans that carry an interest subsidy (PLA) are provided to the HLM associations by a special non-banking institution (Caisse des Dépôts et Consignations, CDC). The CDC takes care of the financing of investments in the public sector and in social housing construction. Thus, the HLM associations do not borrow the money for their new construction activities directly from the capital market. They do put up some of their own equity. According to the Compte du Logement 1996, their assets accounted for 3.2 percent in 1994. For improvement and renovation of dwellings, however, their share was 43.8 percent. In addition, part of the investment costs were subsidized by the government (new construction, 17.2 percent; dwelling improvement, 16.7 percent). To make new construction possible, the HLM associations therefore had to find outside funding for 79.2 percent of the total. This share was only 39.5 percent for dwelling improvement and renovation. Nearly half of these investments are covered by maintenance funds.

The CDC collects capital from savings banks, pension funds, and other financial institutions. At the beginning of the 1990s, 88 percent was derived from savings banks and pension funds; 12 percent was derived from the State (NEI, 1989; Marchal, 1989). The amounts derived from household savings deposits came mainly from the so-called Livret A savings plan. Because the interest rate was low, between four and five percent, households increasingly choose to invest their savings elsewhere. In this way, the supply of savings from the Livret A system declined by 34 million francs between 1989 and 1992, ending up at 52 million francs. By other means, the CDC was nonetheless able to expand the available financial means in this period (Oxley and Smith, 1996, p. 89).

The CDC has the right to review the management of the HLM associations. It has the right to refuse a PLA loan on the grounds of a negative review. Since 1986, the CDC has a monopoly on financing of construction in the social housing sector (Boucher, 1988, p. 313).

If dwellings are built by HLM associations, they are eligible for a PLA loan to cover a minimum of 55 percent and a maximum of 95 percent of the allowable investment costs, depending on which association applies for the loan. The loans are made up of annuities. In 1995, PLA loans were made for a term of 32 to 35 years (the life of the loan is tied to the length of operation of the dwelling). The interest due on these loans is low. It is linked to the interest rate that applies to the home savings scheme: 5.8 percent in 1995, 4.8 percent in 1996 (OTB survey on financing in the social rented sector, 1996). The government's interest subsidy covers the difference between the cost of the loan and the actual amount paid out in interest and installments on the principal. The interest on PLA loans is considerably lower than the interest that HLM associations are supposed to pay on the capital market (8.5 percent in 1995). Lending to HLM associations is not entirely free of risk. This is demonstrated by the fact that HLM associations pay between 1.5 and two percent more interest than the going rates on government bonds. The difference between interest on loans to HLM associations and that on loans to other government bodies, such as municipalities, ranges from one to 1.5 percent (OTB survey on financing in the social rented sector, 1996).

Since the PLA loan covers between 55 and 95 percent of the construction costs, various other loans are needed to top up the financing. One source is the Crédit Foncier France (CUFF). Every loan is secured by savings deposits or bonds and a government subsidy that is provided to the CUFF. The loan conditions diverge slightly from those that apply to PLA loans. For instance, the builder or developer has to cover at least 25 percent of the building costs. And the PLA loan may not be more than 65 percent of the initial construction costs of the dwelling. The rate of interest can be fixed for 25 years or be variable for 30 years. These loans are extended to private parties as well as to HLM associations (Oxley and Smith, 1996, p. 88).

In addition to the PLA loans, rental dwellings can also be financed by funds that are built up through contributions of employers, as in the Comptoir des Entrepreneurs (PEEC). This "patronal" scheme has been in existence since 1953. At that time, it was set up in an attempt to resolve the financing problems related to the recovery from war damage. The required contribution from employers is currently one percent of the gross payroll. The patronal scheme only applies to companies with at least ten employees. Since 1980, the contribution is divided over two funds: 0.53 percent is dedicated to rent subsidies, and 47 percent goes to loans for construction activities. Different organizations are involved in collecting the money. The main ones are the Comités Interprofessionels pour le Logement (CIL), the Chambers of Commerce, and the HLM associations. The loans are made available at extremely low interest rates, but they can only be applied to a maximum of 25 percent of the construction costs. Top-up loans are usually arranged by the municipality and the departements. Furthermore, the financing from this fund is also used as a supplement to financing in the form of PLA loans (Papa, 1992, p. 118; Oxley and Smith, 1996, p. 89).

Besides the financing for the social rented sector, loans can also be extended for the intermediate sector. In this sector, rental and owner-occupancy dwellings are offered to households whose income is too high for the social sector but still have trouble finding a suitable dwelling on the private rented market or the homeowner market. In this context, the CDC provides loans, the Prêts Locatifs Intermédiaires (PLIs) to the HLM and SEM organizations. Construction loans of this type pose conditions for a period of nine years on the amount of rent in relation to the tenant's income. Oxley and Smith (1996, p. 88) give an overview of the financing system in the French social housing sector (Figure 7.1).

Figure 7.1   Financing system in the social rented sector in France

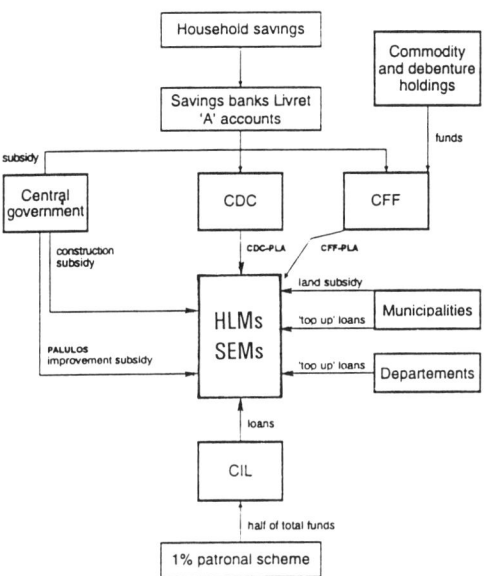

Social housing finance system: France. HLMs (Habitations à Loyer Modéré)(housing at moderate rents): includes both public and private providers of social housing with responsibility for construction and management. SEMs (Sociétés d'Economie Mixte): social housing providers and managers operating under company law and funded from public and private sources. CDCs (Caisse des Dépôts et Consignations): a public funding agency which is the main provider of loans for social housing construction. Financed through savings. CFF (Credit Foncier France): funded through its own holdings and government subsidy in its provision of loans for social housing construction. CIL (Comités Interprofessionels pour le Logement): one of the main agencies responsible for collecting funds from employers under the 1% patronal scheme and reallocating these funds for social housing loans and housing allowances.

Source: Oxley and Smith, 1996, p. 88.

In France too, the annual demand for financing in the social rented sector is closely linked to the volume of the new construction program (Table 7.2). The production of social rental units has been fairly consistent in France over the past years. In contrast to most other countries studied here, production has been rising since the beginning of the 1990s. From 45,000 dwellings in 1990, production rose to 78,000 dwellings in 1994. This increase is due to use of housing construction as an instrument of the anti-cyclical economic policy, as pursued by the French government.

The respondents to our questionnaire expect that the annual production will again reach the level of about 50,000 dwellings in the coming years. The initial costs of a new dwelling in the social rented sector are estimated to be about 400,000 francs (NLG

Table 7.2 Annual development of new construction activities in the social rented sector compared to the total number of housing starts in France, 1980-1995 and the projected production for 1996-1997

	Number of rental housing starts	Number housing starts	Share social rented dwellings (%)
1980	60,300	400,000	15
1985	65,000	295,000	22
1986	60,000	295,000	20
1987	54,000	310,300	17
1988	54,000	327,000	17
1989	50,000	339,400	15
1990	45,800	305,900	15
1991	58,900	309,800	19
1992	63,700	277,000	23
1993	71,400	255,000	28
1994	78,000	-	-
1995	62,000	-	-
1996	50,000	-	-
1997	50,000	-	-

Source: Marchal, 1989, p. 35; European Commission, 1994; OTB survey on financing in the social rented sector, 1996.

133,000) (OTB survey on financing in the social rented sector, 1996). Assuming that 79 percent of the required financial means is borrowed on the capital market, the annual demand for financing comes to roughly 15.8 billion francs (NLG 5,240,000,000).

It should be mentioned that the total amount invested by the HLM associations in 1994 was considerably higher. According to the Compte du Logement 1996, those investments amounted to 50 billion francs (NLG 16,659,000,000) in 1994. These cover all the activities of the HLM organizations. Naturally, part of these investments are subsidized or financed by the organizations' own assets.

7.6 Risk and guarantees in the social rented sector

The HLM associations are highly diverse in terms of size, financial activities, volume of holdings, and geographic territory. Accordingly, the risk profile is diverse as well. The organizations operate at both the municipal and the regional level. They are closely aligned with political interests, as demonstrated by the fact that many members of parliament are also on the board of an HLM. These boards consist of individuals who are nominated by the préfet of the departement and by other organizations (including municipalities, savings banks, and tenants). The HLM associations collaborate at the regional level. At the national level, the organizations are joined in the Union Nationale des Fédérations d'Organismes d'HLM (UNFOHLM).

In the 1980s in particular, several HLM organizations ran into financial trouble. Their problems were caused by a combination of vacancy, rent arrears, and an obsolescent housing stock. According to Boucher (1988, p. 316), between 35 and 49 percent of the HLM associations were in financial straits. In 1984, a member of UNFOHLM, Cornaire, explained their financial difficulties. The first reason was a mismatch of supply and demand on the market for social rented housing. For instance, the dwellings built in the past were mainly large flats for families with numerous offspring. But in the 1980s, the demand for rented dwellings was mainly for small units. Moreover, large dwellings were often too expensive for the small households. Another reason was that in the past, the HLM associations devoted little or no attention to marketing aspects when developing their residential construction projects. They built dwellings wherever they could get a cheap building site, without investigating the local demand for housing. Moreover, in most cases, little attention was given to adequate traffic planning to make the development accessible. By the 1990s, the problems in these areas, known as the grands ensembles, have only increased. The research bureau Banlieuscopies even called for some kind of Marshall Plan to pull the suburban population out of the doldrums (Venema, 1994). According to this research bureau, the problems of these suburbs are not high on the political agenda of either the left or the right.

The financial problems confronting the HLM associations have not been resolved in the 1990s either. The respondents to our questionnaire indicated that over five percent of the HLM associations had run into financial trouble over the past several years. Notably, these difficulties led to hardly any cases of bankruptcy. Furthermore, the respondents said that the financial management of the HLM associations is not always optimal. They indicated that the financial management lies somewhere between bookkeeping practices and a method by which the financial management and risk assessment are fully integrated in the way the entire organization is run. In order to overcome the financial obstacles, the sale of social-rented dwellings has recently been taken up in France. The sales are coordinated by the umbrella organization of landlords, which is supervised by the central government and the préfet (Ghékiere, 1993). Strict rules and guidelines have been formulated for the sale of rented dwellings. In contrast to Belgium and England, for example, French law does not recognize the tenant's right to buy.

Guarantees for separate loans
When an HLM association wants to close a subsidized loan, the organization is required to participate in a guarantee system. This system operates like an insurance policy, which comes into effect when an HLM cannot meet its financial obligations. The Ministry of Construction and the Ministry of Finance are contractually bound to assume financial responsibility for the loans. In return, the HLM periodically pays a lump-sum amount to the Caisse de Garantie du Logement Social (CGLS). The contribution consists of a fixed percentage of the loan, which differs among the various organizations involved. The guarantee institution for the social rented sector is operated by the CDC and is under the supervision of an administrative council. Both the PLA and the PALULOS loans are intended for the HLMs that are in financial difficulty. Those loans are guaranteed by the CGLS (Oxley and Smith, 1996, p. 90).

7.7 Opportunities for outside lenders

In France, social landlords draw loans for new construction and renovation activities from special financing institutions. In that light, there are hardly any opportunities for outside lenders to extend loans to individual HLM associations. It is possible to participate in the financing of the social rented sector in France, though indirectly, through loans to the Caisse des Dépôts et Consignations (CDC). The CDC has a monopoly position with regard to the financing of social rented dwellings. The CDC accumulates its capital by way of savings banks, pension funds, and other financial institutions.

Making loans to HLM associations for other activities is not entirely free of risk. Relatively many HLM associations have become insolvent in the past few years. The fact that lending entails some risk is also demonstrated by the difference between the interest on government loans and the interest on loans to HLM associations. The respondents to the OTB survey on financing in the social rented sector estimate that difference to be roughly two percent.

8
SWEDEN

P.J. Boelhouwer

8.1 Introduction

Sweden occupies a very special position among the seven countries considered in this study. Not only is the structure of the Swedish housing market different, but the changes that have taken place within it over the past several years are unparalleled in Western Europe. Until the early 1990s, the Swedish government had a firm grip on the housing market. Housing policy was dominated by the Social Democratic Party, which was almost continuously in power. But the fairy tale came to an abrupt end. The wave of privatization that was instigated at the start of the decade combined with the towering problems that arose on the Swedish financial markets in the autumn of 1992 brought this chapter to a close. The climax was the crash in both the mortgage market and the housing market. For example, between April 1991 and October 1992, the price of an owner-occupied dwelling in Stockholm dropped by 18 percent (Englund, 1993) while the mortgage interest rate shot up. Compared to the previous year, investment in the housing market declined by 6.2 percent in 1992 and by 35 percent in 1993. The figures for 1994 are expected to show a decline in investment by 38 percent (Van de Ven, 1995, p. 120).

The tenure-neutral housing policy that was introduced in 1974 is unique in Western Europe. Many of the countries studied here, including the Netherlands, purport to follow such a policy. But Sweden alone applies this principle consistently in every instance of government intervention. The aim of that policy is not to shunt households into a particular tenure sector. Instead, the aim is to give all households the maximum freedom of choice, regardless of their income level. The occupants of similar dwellings in different tenure classes should ultimately incur the same housing costs. However, it should be noted that according to Swedish regulations, dwellings in multi-family structures can only be operated as rentals or cooperatives. For this reason, the freedom of choice is not really optimal in practice. Furthermore, the tenure-neutral policy implies that virtually all housing production and renovation could count on government subsidies -- until recently, that is.

Another situation unique to Sweden is the way of setting rents on the basis of use value. This calculation takes four characteristics into account: collective negotiations (tenants and landlord agree on a maximum rent increase), the price-leader role of the

Table 8.1   Swedish housing stock by tenure, 1992, percentages

Number x 1,000	Owner-occupiers	Cooperatives	Private commercial rented sector	Non-profit rented sector	Other
4,042	43	16	17	22	2

Source: SCB, 1992; Van de Ven, 1995, p. 118.

non-profit sector, the opportunity for non-profit landlords to apply their rent revenues to their own dwelling stock, and the principle of equal rent for comparable dwellings (Van de Ven, 1995, p. 132).

Table 8.1 gives insight into the distribution of the housing stock over the various tenure classes.

The Swedish housing stock comprises roughly four million dwellings. Of that total, 2.1 million are flats and 1.9 million are either single-family or two-family houses. Sweden recognizes four tenure classes: owner-occupiers, renters in the non-profit sector, renters in the private sector, and tenant-owners. The last of these four classes is better known as the cooperative sector. The owner-occupiers live in 43 percent of the housing stock, the non-profit rented sector accounts for 22 percent, the private rented sector has grown to 17 percent, and 16 percent is owned by cooperatives.

As pointed out above, the diverse tenures in Sweden are clearly separated with regard to type of dwelling. Rentals and coops are found almost exclusively in multi-family structures. Owner-occupancy is found solely in single-family houses. Swedish law only allows rentals in multi-family buildings. Home ownership is inextricably bound up with ownership of land. Thus, a person can own an entire building but not part of it.

In Sweden, flats and apartments comprise 54 percent of the housing stock (SCB, 1992). This is an outcome of the policy prevailing from 1964 to 1974. That was the time of the One Million Dwellings Program. Throughout Europe, housing production was predominantly in highrise buildings. For the sake of comparison, flats and apartments make up only 30 percent of the housing stock in the Netherlands.

8.2 The institutional structure

The social rented sector in Sweden is in the hands of the municipal non-profit housing associations. There are just over 300 of them, and they differ considerably from one another. Their holdings vary from about 20 dwellings to more than 50,000 (Wiktorin, 1992). Over half of these organizations have fewer than 2,000 dwellings.

The board of directors of a non-profit housing association is appointed by the city council. Swedish municipalities are efficient, by European standards, and have considerable freedom in making policy. The municipalities can levy taxes and determine where and when construction should take place. The composition of the board of the municipal housing associations is a mirror of local political relations. Previously, the board consisted mainly of politically astute individuals, but the current tendency is to allow persons with a financial background to take part as well. This is supposed to enhance the professionalism of the board (Lindencrona, 1994).

Usually, each municipality has one housing association. Large cities may have more than one non-profit landlord, however. The task of the municipal housing associations is to operate housing on a non-profit basis. In Sweden, everyone is eligible for non-profit rented units (mostly flats). There are no restrictions on income.

Most of the units rented out by municipal housing associations are modern flats; 71 percent were built after 1960. Similarly, the majority of the dwellings operated by these landlords are in multi-family buildings. Only three percent are single-family houses. The apartments are in lowrise buildings of two or three stories. Over the past few years, single-family houses, many with a small garden, have also been built in the non-profit sector. In 1990 and 1991, ten percent of the new non-profit dwellings were single-family houses. Most of the dwellings (75 percent) in the municipal non-profit sector have two or three rooms. Studio units and large flats (with four or more rooms) are more prevalent in the private commercial sector than in the non-profit sector (Hägred, 1993).

The non-profit sector in Sweden serves all segments of the population. No maximum is set on income levels. Therefore, the non-profit rented sector should not be equated with the social rented sector as it exists in many other West European countries.

Nearly all municipal housing associations are affiliated with the interest group SABO (Swedish Federation of Municipal Housing Associations). This group operates 900,000 apartments and has a total of 1.5 million tenants, which amounts to one-fifth of the entire population (Lindencrona, 1994).

8.3 Supervision

The operation of non-profit housing associations is supervised by the municipality. Ultimately, the State and the municipal government provide a backup in the event the landlords would be unable to meet their financial obligations (OTB survey on financing in the social rented sector, 1996). In fact, these municipal housing associations can be counted as part of the public sector. In this respect, Sweden differs from most of the other West European countries, where private organizations are responsible for the non-profit rental sector.

8.4 Subsidies for the non-profit rented sector

Object subsidies and operating subsidies
As mentioned in the introduction, practically no housing in Sweden is either built or

remodeled without government subsidy. In all tenure sectors, and for new construction as well as improvements on existing dwellings, the Swedish government applies a system of interest subsidies. Until 1993, the subsidy for rented dwellings was highest in the first year. After that, the subsidy was decreased incrementally over the next 20 years. In the first year, the interest rate was set at 3.4 percent. The difference between this fixed rate and the going market rate was compensated. After the first year, the fixed rate increased gradually; each year it was raised by 0.375 percent.

In January 1993, a new system of interest subsidies came into force. The rationale was to reduce government outlays for housing subsidies. The subsidy period was cut back to ten years. The government wanted better protection against fluctuations in interest rates. Since then, the interest subsidy in the first year covers 57 percent of the calculated interest costs of a dwelling built in 1993. After that, the subsidy is reduced by four percent per year. For dwellings started in 1994, the interest subsidy covers 54 percent of the calculated interest costs. Also for these dwellings, the subsidy is lowered each year by four percent. For dwellings built in 1995, the initial subsidies are reduced even further, and so forth. The interest costs are calculated on the basis of standardized investment costs. They depend on the size of the dwelling. Units larger than 120 square meters get no subsidy (Bengtsson, 1994).

The State has done away with the interest subsidies sooner than the municipal housing associations anticipated. Therefore, these associations have run into financial problems. Most problems are encountered by housing associations that have built extensively over the past decade and have a small stock of older dwellings. Because of the rising rents and the economic recession, the demand for dwellings has declined. In 1993, there was a three-percent vacancy rate in the rental stock operated by the municipal housing associations. Vacancies were rare before that time. The vacancies are concentrated in thinly populated areas and pose enormous problems for certain housing associations (SABO, 1993; Van de Ven, 1995, p. 124).

Rent subsidy and rent-setting
Two forms of rent subsidy exist in Sweden. One is targeted toward retirees, the other primarily toward low-income families with children. For both forms, the national government has formulated rules, while the municipalities take charge of allocation. Of all tenants, 33 percent receive a rent subsidy (1992). About 36 percent of all retired persons and 24 percent of the households with children receive a rent subsidy. Of the households with three or more children, 55 percent get a rent subsidy. In 1991, the expenditure amounted to SKr 13 billion, which translates to over NLG 3 billion (Bengtsson, 1994, p. 193). The government outlays for subsidies to retirees are especially high. Homebuyers are also eligible for a housing expenditure subsidy. In 1991, 21 percent of all households received some form of housing expenditure subsidy; this share rose to 25 percent in 1993.

As mentioned above, the Swedish system of rent-setting is definitely unique by European standards. The annual rent increase in Sweden is determined in negotiations between the tenants (as represented in the National Federation of Tenants Associations, the Hyresgästernas Riksförbund) and the non-profit landlords (the municipal housing associations and the umbrella organization SABO). In this manner, each autumn, the municipal housing associations and the local representatives of the tenants jointly set the rent ceiling for the next year.

The system of collective rent negotiations was codified in the Rent Negotiations Act of 1978. The ceiling agreed upon by the tenants and landlords is also binding for the commercial rented sector. The non-profit sector determines the rents. Only when the non-profit landlords have agreed on a new rent level with their tenants can the annual negotiations begin in the commercial sector (SABO, 1993).

In preparation for the negotiations, the municipal landlords calculate the real costs that should be covered by rent revenues. The housing association submits a budget for the next year, showing the projected costs and income. This budget specifies the costs for each complex and for the corporation as a whole. The calculation of costs is based on the anticipated expense of capital, depreciation, maintenance, insurance, management, and vacancy. It also includes the costs of heating, garbage collection, and electricity. And last but not least, the calculations include reimbursement of the costs incurred by the local tenants association for taking part in the negotiations. There are no long-term reserves for maintenance or any other funds. On the income side, a calculation is made that includes the rents, interest, coverage for service costs, and subsidies. This results in the required average rent increase (Van Harten and Wilke, 1993). In this way, rents in the non-profit rented sector are based on real costs. The landlords do not make any profit.

In the course of negotiations, the local tenants association can raise objections to the calculated costs, for instance, or the efficiency of the organization. This means that the local tenants association can negotiate with the housing association over the total rent level, over the spread of costs across the stock, and over the services that the housing association must provide in return for the rent at the amount set (SABO, 1993).

It is conceivable that the local parties may not be able to reach an agreement. In that event, the SABO and the National Federation of Tenants Associations set the rents. This task is performed by the Rent Market Committee. The utility-value rent plays a key role at this point. In case tenants and landlords have a difference of opinion about how high the rent should be, the rent must be set at a fair or reasonable level. The Rent Act stipulates that the rent is not considered reasonable if it is substantially higher than the rent charged for non-profit dwellings with the same utility value.

The municipal housing associations may resort to rent pooling, an internal leveling mechanism, on new and old dwellings. The older dwellings thus become more expensive than they would be if strictly based on production costs. By the same token, the new dwellings become relatively less expensive.

The annual negotiations on rent increases previously set the rents for the entire municipal housing stock. At present, they are set for each complex. This is a more market-oriented approach. In this manner, it is easier to differentiate the stock by its quality (Lindencrona, 1994).

There are some drawbacks to the rent differentiation, however. Deprived population groups might become concentrated in the lower-quality parts of the stock, since those dwellings are less expensive. This may promote the creation of ghettos. For this reason, tenants associations are against rent differentiation. Another drawback is that residents of the better parts of the stock are confronted with a higher rent increase than residents of lower-quality dwellings. Because of the differentiation, the rent increase ceiling turns out to be higher than it would with an average rent increase (Van de Ven, 1995, p. 125).

8.5 Financing in the non-profit rented sector

Until 1991, the government provided long-term loans for the highest risk part of the investment in the non-profit rented sector. The government loans financed the top 25 to 30 percent of the investment in new construction. The share depended on the tenure of the dwellings. This constituted the second mortgage. Up to 70 percent of the costs of production could be borrowed on the capital market through special mortgage institutions; this constituted the first mortgage. All but one of these special institutions are owned by banks. The loans were provided at market interest rates. In this way, private parties were able to get financing to cover 95 percent of the costs. The municipal housing corporations could finance up to 100 percent of the costs. The second mortgage was only available for dwellings with initial costs under a certain maximum (Papa, 1992, p. 131).

Until 1 July 1985, these second mortgages appeared directly on the government budget. Indeed, people called them government loans. On 1 July 1985, this financing was transferred to a separate financing institution, namely the Statens Bostadsfinansieringsaktiebolag (SBAB), which is owned by the State. The SBAB extends long-term loans to individuals and organizations to finance housing construction and improvement projects that have been approved by the State. The SBAB provided the second mortgage for nearly all these projects. Because these mortgages are subsidized, the first mortgages are eligible for subsidy as well. The SBAB obtains the required capital by issuing bonds on the capital market. The principal buyers of such bonds are institutional investors and banks. Interest rates on these bonds are adjusted annually. Therefore, the interest rates on the loans for housing construction and/or improvement have to be adjusted each year too. It should be noted that the SBAB passes the loans on to other borrowers at the same interest rate as it paid to obtain the capital, though adding an administrative surcharge (Boleat, 1987, p. 30). Since 1989, the SBAB is allowed to issue its bonds in foreign markets. In 1993, roughly one-third of the "funding" came from foreign capital. This share is expected to grow to 50 percent in the future. The responsibility for allocation of the government loans lies with the National Board of Housing, Building and Planning and with the County Housing Boards that resort under the National Board.

Until 1990, an SBAB loan was required to become eligible for the interest subsidies on the first and second mortgage. In December 1990, however, the Swedish parliament abolished this monopoly. Then, other mortgage institutions could offer to arrange this part of the financing, and the SBAB could start to extend first mortgages too. The

SBAB was subsequently transformed into a normal mortgage institution (Papa, 1992, p. 133).

In 1992, parliament decided to completely revise the system of financing for the housing market. Since that year, money for investments in housing production and renovation has to be borrowed entirely on the capital market. The lion's share of the loans is arranged by mortgage banks. General banks arrange 20 percent of the loans (OTB survey on financing in the social rented sector, 1996). The mortgage banks act as intermediaries between the non-profit landlords and the lenders, such as the pension funds. In 90 percent of the transactions, the loans are annuities; only 10 percent are linear loans. These loans have to be paid off in either 40 or 50 years. Thus, they are arranged for the whole period during which the housing will be operated. The interest rate is adjusted periodically; usually, the period of adjustment is between one and five years.

The State guarantees the portion of the loan with the highest risk, which covers between 25 and 30 percent of the production costs. A premium is charged for the guarantee. Without this risk insurance, it is impossible to arrange 100-percent financing on the capital market. It should be kept in mind that, on average, more than 95 percent of the investment costs are financed from outside sources. Furthermore, the amount of equity is generally limited. The figures mentioned by respondents to the questionnaire ranged from two to five percent. The small share of equity reflects the fact that it is difficult for the institutions to build up their own assets, as explained earlier in the discussion of rent-setting. The loans on the capital market are not only taken out for new construction. They are also arranged to cover a large number of other activities. These include maintenance and improvement, urban renewal, and, among other things, the acquisition and sale of property (OTB survey on financing in the social rented sector, 1996). The respondents to the OTB survey had various opinions on whether enough capital was available for the non-profit institutions. Their answers ranged from "there are more than sufficient financial means available for all institutions" to "only the financially strong social landlords have a chance to arrange loans." However, the umbrella organization for non-profit landlords (SABO) indicated that enough capital is available in Sweden. According to this organization, the average interest rate for loans that non-profit organizations arranged on the capital market in 1995 is 10.73 percent. The interest-écart, or the difference relative to the government loans, amounted to 1.73 percent. Thus, the interest-écart is considerably higher than the average for the Netherlands, which is 0.25 percent. The real interest rate is high too. Thus, the inflation in Sweden will probably be 2.75 percent, which implies a real interest rate of about eight percent.

The subsidies in housing construction will most likely be diminished in the future. The capital market is in a period of crisis. Banks encounter increasing risk in lending money. In this context, the cost of capital rises. It is expected that real estate prices will continue to decline in the coming years, while the interest will remain at a high level and perhaps even increase. The production of new housing will also be limited in the next several years (Bengtsson, 1994).

As pointed out above, since the large-scale privatization wave of the early 1990s, the market for mortgages and housing has collapsed. Between April 1991 and October 1992, the price of an owner-occupied dwelling in Stockholm dropped by 18 percent (Englund, 1993) and mortgage interest rates shot upwards. Investment in the housing market declined relative to the previous year by 6.2 percent in 1992 and by 35 percent in 1993. It was expected that investment would decline by 38 percent in 1994. The production of housing is still very low in all sectors. There were only 10,000 new housing starts in 1993 (Hägred, 1994).

The SABO does not expect the production level to rise before the year 2000 for the simple reason that production costs have risen dramatically. In 1993, a new non-profit rental dwelling with two bedrooms cost roughly NLG 1,275 per month. Yet the same dwelling in the existing stock was supposed to rent for about NLG 800 per month (SABO, 1993). In response to the OTB survey, the SABO representative indicated that the cost of building a non-profit rental dwelling with an average size of 71.4 square meters had gone up in the meantime. In 1996, that dwelling would cost SKr 884,000 (NLG 225,000). A more spacious dwelling of 100 square meters runs about one million Swedish krona (NLG 250,000). This covers the total initial costs, including the cost of construction, land, local taxes, and development. The steep drop in new construction is evident in Table 8.2. The SABO expects new construction to level off in the coming years at about 5,000 dwellings, which is low for Sweden too.

Table 8.2 Annual development of new construction activities in the non-profit rented sector compared to the total number of completed dwellings in Sweden, 1980-1995 and the projected production for 1996-1997

	Number completions non-profit rental dwellings	Number completions	Share non-profit rental dwellings (%)
1980	13,400	51,400	48
1985	9,200	32,900	29
1986	8,600	28,800	30
1987	8,900	30,700	30
1988	11,700	40,600	29
1989	13,000	50,000	26
1990	14,600	58,400	25
1991	15,400	66,900	23
1992	15,500	57,300	27
1993	9,500	35,100	27
1994	8,200	-	-
1995	4,900	-	-
1996	4,400	-	-
1997	5,000	-	-

Source: Menkveld, 1993, p. 108; European Commission, 1994; OTB survey on financing in the social rented sector, 1996.

8.6 Risk and guarantees

Tenants have an influential position in Sweden, as mentioned earlier. Annual rent adjustments are based on negotiations between landlords and tenants. The Swedish system of negotiated rents does have a drawback. The non-profit housing associations are hardly able to build up any reserves for maintenance. Thus, the financing of upkeep may be in jeopardy. The reason is that the rents are determined in the course of negotiations over the budget based on real costs incurred by the landlord. The Tenants Association does not approve of reserving money for long-term maintenance. In practice, the only deferred expenditures that are included in the negotiations are reserves for painting and decorating and the replacement of appliances, especially kitchen equipment, that can be depreciated over a period of ten to 15 years. Thus, no reserves are built up for renovation or replacement of the dwelling (Koopman, 1992). This practice is reflected in the solvability of the non-profit associations: in Sweden, between six and seven percent; in the Netherlands, about 12 percent (Van Harten and Wilke, 1993). Early in the 1990s, analysts in Sweden expected that the lack of reserves, in combination with the termination of low-interest government loans, would lead to trouble in the future (Van de Ven, 1995, p. 128). In the meantime, this expectation has come to pass, according to information from the SABO. This umbrella organization estimates that between one and five percent of the non-profit landlords have run into financial difficulties over the last several years (OTB survey on financing in the social rented sector, 1996). There have not been any cases of bankruptcy, however. As mentioned above in the discussion of oversight, this is closely connected to the fact that the State and the municipality ultimately guarantee the non-profit landlords. Actually, the non-profit landlords are not private organizations, as they are in most of the West European countries reviewed here. Instead, performing as municipal housing associations, they may be considered part of the public sector. According to most of the respondents to our survey, the financial problems of the non-profit landlords are not due to poor management. The respondents state that the financial management and the risk analysis are fully integrated in the operations of the whole organization.

8.7 Opportunities for outside lenders

In light of the information presented above, we may conclude that the Swedish non-profit associations are headed for hard times. The hefty government subsidies that had been provided for decades have been cut back sharply. Housing demand has declined, and maintenance and improvement will require serious attention. In order to address this situation, the organizations have expanded their range of activities. Whereas they had previously concentrated on renting accommodation, they are now providing all kinds of services related to housing and they are making efforts to improve the residential environment. The financial picture for most non-profit associations is bleak, however. The problem is that they have not been in a good position to build up the necessary financial reserves. All in all, the solvability of most landlords is weak.

Nonetheless, this low level of solvency should not prevent outside lenders from offering loans to the non-profit associations. The municipal housing associations are actually public organizations with the full backing of the local government. Thus, the lenders would run little risk. In this case, then, a high level of solvency is not imperative. The financing is derived directly from the capital market, and the only intermediaries involved are mortgage banks. On that basis, the institutional structure should not form an obstacle either. Furthermore, the possible returns are relatively high. For one thing, the loans arranged by the non-profit associations on the capital market in 1995 carried an average interest rate of 10.73 percent. Since inflation will probably be running 2.75 percent in 1997, the real interest rate will be roughly eight percent.

On the other hand, the extremely low production of new housing in Sweden --not even 5,000 dwellings per year-- means that there is no big market awaiting newcomers. At an average initial cost of NLG 225,000 and an investment of five percent in equity, this implies that the non-profit associations in Sweden will borrow roughly NLG 1,068,750,000 for new construction activities each year. These loans will be arranged directly or indirectly on the capital market. More opportunities may lie in the financing of maintenance and improvement activities. For the most part, the stock of non-profit rented dwellings in Sweden was built between 1964 and 1974. Since then, the dwellings have become somewhat outdated. However, there is little insight as yet in the demand for financing that their obsolescence will generate.

In sum, we definitely see opportunities for outside lenders to take part in the financing of the activities of Sweden's non-profit landlords. Although the scope of the market is limited, the risks are low and the returns on the loans are reasonably high.

9
SUMMARY

P.J. Boelhouwer

9.1 Introduction

The central topic of this report is the means by which the financing of the social rented sector --also called the non-profit rented sector-- is arranged in seven countries in Western Europe. These are the Netherlands, Belgium, Denmark, Germany, England, France, and Sweden. The report also devotes attention to the way in which the social rented sector is organized in these countries. The objective of the investigation is to draw a general picture of each of the countries studied. That picture should provide sufficient insight to determine whether or not the various countries would be of interest to outside lenders. A more detailed analysis of those countries that show enough potential investment opportunities could be carried out in a follow-up study. Given that objective, the following ten research questions were formulated.

1. How was the institutional structure of the social rented sector designed in the seven countries under study?
2. In what way does the government provide financial support to the social rented sector in the form of subsidies that are tied to either the tenants or the dwellings and what fiscal advantages, if any, does the government offer?
3. What form does the public control over management by social landlords take in the seven countries?
4. How is the financing of new construction and renovation activities undertaken by social landlords arranged in the seven countries?
5. What risks and guarantees pertain to the social rented sector in the seven countries?
6. What conditions are set on giving loans to social landlords in the seven countries and what risks can be identified?
7. What is the estimated volume of the annual financing need among social landlords for the production of new dwellings in the seven countries?
8. How do the interest rates for loans to social landlords compare among the seven countries?

9. Which lenders to social landlords are active in the countries under study and what is their market share?
10. Which countries in Western Europe are of interest to outside lenders?

This summary reviews the answers to these research questions in consecutive order.

9.2 The institutional structure

When comparing the institutional structure of the social rented sector in the seven countries under study, the most striking finding is the great discrepancy between the actual tenure profile and the social housing objectives. Social rented dwellings are managed not only by private (non-profit) organizations but also by public agencies (usually municipalities). Some countries even combine the two types of management. In Sweden and England, the municipality plays the biggest role as manager of all (Sweden) or a large proportion (England) of the social rented stock. In all the other countries, private non-profit organizations play a key role in the social rented sector. But the municipalities are also active in the social rented sector in those countries, though in the main their role is more modest. In the Netherlands, part of the social rented sector is operated by municipal housing agencies. In Germany, this is done by an organization that is affiliated to the municipality. In Belgium, France, and Denmark, local authorities exert considerable influence as shareholders in (parts of) the social rented sector. It is striking to note what an important role private organizations or individuals play in Germany's social rented sector. In fact, the distinction between the social and the private (commercial) rented sector in Germany is not based on who owns the property but on whether or not the dwelling (still) falls under the social rental regime. In Germany, social rented dwellings may be operated by private parties seeking to make a profit as well as be non-profit organizations. When the period covered by subsidy is over, these dwellings fall under the rental regime of the private rented sector. They subsequently can be sold without restrictions.

With the exception of Sweden and Denmark, the social rented sector is intended to serve households with a low to modal income. In this sense, England puts a strong emphasis on serving low-income households. In catering to the lower incomes, eligibility criteria are applied with respect to the allocation of social rented dwellings. The eligibility criteria, which are mainly based on income, are generally not set by the social landlords. Rather, this is a task of the central, regional, or local government. Actually, there is not really a social rented sector in Sweden and Denmark. The term non-profit rented sector is more appropriate. The dwellings in this sector are accessible to all layers of the population. Even the high-income groups are not excluded from the allocation procedures for dwellings in this sector.
It is not only the tenure structure and the objective of the non-profit rented sector that varies among the seven countries studied. The size of the sector also varies widely (Table 9.1).

Table 9.1 Distribution of the dwelling stock by tenure sector in seven West European countries at the beginning of the 1990s, percentages

	Owner-occupied sector	Private rented sector	Social rented sector	Cooperative sector	Other/ unknown
Netherlands	46	13	40	-	1
Belgium	65	28	6	-	1
England	68	10	22	-	-
Denmark	56	19	21	5	-
Germany	40	40	20	-	-
France	56	21	17	-	6
Sweden	43	17	22	16	2

Source: see chapters on the respective countries.

Of the countries studied, Belgium has by far the smallest non-profit rented sector. That sector accounts for a mere six percent of the country's dwelling stock. This is not surprising, as the Belgian government has promoted the owner-occupied sector for years. Under the stimulus of this policy, low-income groups and especially families with children can count on government subsidies. Many low-income groups in Belgium are forced to rent in the private rented sector. In Denmark, Germany, and France, the non-profit rented sector comprises about one-fifth of the dwelling stock. It is true that these countries support the development of this sector. But at the same time, they assign the private sector an important function too. In Denmark, there is a deliberate choice for owner-occupancy. In France and particularly in Germany, people favor the private rented sector. The Netherlands is exceptional in Western Europe, with 40 percent of the stock in the social rented sector. Unlike the situation in other countries, housing production in the Netherlands was predominantly in the social rented sector up till the early 1990s. In part, this special position can be explained by the pervasive housing shortage in this country. In most of the other countries, the housing market was already saturated by the 1970s or the early 1980s.

9.3 Financial support from the government

Generally speaking, the government has retreated from the housing market in many West European countries in deference to the free play of supply and demand. This usually implies a reduction in the financial support for the social rented sector. As a consequence, the rents increase. In addition, the operating risks are increasingly passed on to the social landlord, who then has to adopt a more market-oriented approach.

Object subsidies
In all seven countries studied, the non-profit rented sector still has some form of object subsidy. However, in many countries, the volume of those subsidies has declined during the past decade. In the Netherlands, for instance, since 1995, no more generic object subsidies have been granted to build social rented dwellings. The municipalities are still able to provide limited amounts in the form of a lump sum. Social landlords can invest part of their assets, should they so desire, to finance the construction of new social rented dwellings. Sweden has been terminating object subsidies at an accelerated pace since 1993. Moreover, the fiscal advantages for the municipal housing companies were revoked in 1992. In Denmark, the construction of social housing has been subsidized since 1982 by way of subsidies on the interest paid on indexed loans. Until 1990, the subsidies on interest fully covered the interest on the indexed loans. However, in 1990, the term of the loans was extended from 35.5 years to 50.5 years. This brought the annual repayment of principal down to a lower level than previously. In this way, some room was created to pay part of the interest costs out of the rental income.

In England, new construction by the local authorities was cut back sharply in the 1980s. The government's Housing Investment Programme indicates how much the local authorities are allowed to invest. In addition, the English government de-linked the municipal housing operation of the local authorities from the income derived from municipal taxation. In doing so, the local authorities lost the opportunity to make use of these funds for financing or for keeping rents from rising too much. Furthermore, the Right to Buy was still removing dwellings from the stock held by the municipalities. Over the past few years, housing associations have had to turn to the capital market for an increasing share of the financing they need for new construction.

In Belgium, France, and Germany, state support for the construction of non-profit rented dwellings has increased slightly over the past several years. It is starting to recover after the retreat of government in the 1970s and 1980s and in the wake of a sharp drop in new construction in the social rented sector. In the 1980s, the production of new social rented dwellings in Belgium had declined to a few hundred units per year. In order to give the sector new impetus, an emergency program entitled Domus Flandria was started in 1993 in the province of Flanders. This plan envisages the construction of 10,000 social rented dwellings through public-private cooperation. In France, government support for the non-profit rented sector forms part of a program started in 1993 for investment in real estate. The main objectives of this program are to create jobs, to buttress investors' confidence, and to reduce vacancies. Besides building 190,000 social rented dwellings, the plan also entails the construction of 110,000 owner-occupancy dwellings in the social sector and the renovation of 200,000 social rented dwellings.

In Germany, a considerable housing shortage emerged at the end of the 1980s. This was partly due to reunification and the immigration that accompanied that process. When the shortage came to light, a new building program known as the Third Way (3. Förderungsweg) was started. This subsidy provision was changed in 1994. Since then, besides a fixed basic subsidy, there is also a supplementary subsidy. The latter is dependent on the renter's income and household composition. The reason to make this change is to put the subsidy money to more efficient use.

It is striking that these three countries --Belgium, France, and Germany-- have had an increase in the government support for construction of new social rented dwellings while the opportunities for social rented dwellings to leak out of the social rented sector (through sale to sitting tenants or by termination of the social bond) have not been restricted (in Belgium); indeed, these options have even been expanded (in Germany and France).

Subject subsidies
In all of the countries studied, subsidy on rent plays an important role in compensating outlays for housing by households in the lower income groups. Almost all countries provide rent subsidies to the occupants of both the non-profit rented sector and the for-profit rented sector. Belgium is the one exception. Renters in the for-profit sector there have no right to rent subsidy. Renters in the non-profit rented sector do receive a subsidy on their rent, in balance. This is not in the form of a payment to the renter, however, as is the practice in the other countries. Instead, the rent is calculated for each individual case on the basis of the household income.

In England, a distinction is made between renters who get income support (welfare benefits) and renters without these benefits. Among the latter, when the amount of rent subsidy is determined, the amount of rent owed and the income of the household are taken into account. In principle, the former receive a rent subsidy (housing benefit) amounting to 100 percent of the "eligible rent" (which is the reasonable rent). This is how people fall into the poverty trap. Their income will have to rise well above the level of welfare if they are to end up with any more money net, after deducting the rent subsidy.

In France, there are three types of subject subsidies. The general rule for rent subsidy (Aide Personalisée au Logement, APL) only applies to people living in dwellings that were built after 1977. In the for-profit sector, another condition is that the renter must have signed a contract with the state. This refers to the so-called regulated rented sector. The other two subsidy regulations are extensions of social welfare and of the support for (young) families with children or family members requiring care.

9.4 Supervision and audit of non-profit sector

In all seven countries studied, forms of supervision and control have been developed in the course of time. These measures pertain to the way the non-profit institutions perform. The reason to develop such measures is that the government considers itself to be responsible to some extent for the provision of housing for low-income groups. Furthermore, the government has provided many subsidies to the landlords. In the Netherlands, France, England (with the exception of the housing associations), and Sweden, the supervision is first and foremost the task of the municipality. Whether or not it is decided to intervene in the management of a housing association in the Netherlands is ultimately up to the state. In France, on the contrary, the regional representative of the state, the préfet, holds sway. In view of the fact that Sweden and England have municipal housing authorities, it is no surprise that control over these companies is carried out by the town council.

In Belgium and England, supervision is carried out by an intermediary umbrella organization, namely the regional Housing Society and the Housing Corporation. In Belgium, however, local building contractors ultimately fall under the supervision of the regional government. The regional Housing Society takes care of the daily supervision. The supervision of the non-profit institutions in Denmark, in contrast, is spread over a number of parties, as befits a social democracy. These parties are the municipality, the personnel, and the renters.

The country where supervision is by far the least developed is Germany. This is in part related to the fact that non-profit rented dwellings can also be rented out by private parties. The landlords of non-profit rented dwellings are only obliged to comply with the subsidy conditions. Those non-profit landlords who are affiliated with the Gesamtverband der Wohnungswirtschaft (GdW) do fall under the supervision of this umbrella organization. Because of the great diversity among the landlords who rent out social rented dwellings, the task of supervision is difficult. This problem drew attention when the biggest non-profit landlord in Germany, called Neue Heimat, went bankrupt at the end of the 1980s.

9.5 Financing in the non-profit rented sector: source of funding

The role of the government in providing loans to finance new non-profit rented dwellings has all but disappeared in the seven West European countries under study. Germany is the only country that still offers the opportunity to take out an interest-free government loan. This loan would cover part of the necessary financing and is only available for dwellings that are subsidized under the first subsidy system (1. Förderungsweg). In all of the countries except England, a portion of the required financing comes from own funds (Table 9.2).

Especially in Germany (33 percent) but also in Belgium (20 percent), a significant share of the financing of new construction is drawn from the social landlords' own funds. Besides their own assets that they put in, part of the financing costs are covered by lump-sum government subsidies. These are only the lump-sum subsidies that are paid out at the time the buildings are put into operation and pertain to the financing. In addition, some countries also have long-term operating subsidies, such as interest subsidies. The subsidies that are received in the course of operation --as in Sweden and Denmark, for instance-- are significantly higher than the amount received at the time operation is started up. Thus, the share of subsidies is often more than 50 percent of the original costs of construction. In the Netherlands, only lump-sum subsidies are still granted, as of January 1, 1995, which puts this country in a very special position. England is the country where the share of the financing costs covered by lump-sum subsidies is the highest (42 percent), compared to the others. But such contributions also play a major role in the financing of new residential construction in Belgium (21 percent), Germany (18 percent), and France (17 percent). The opposite is true in the Netherlands. There, the share of financing that is provided in the form of lump-sum subsidies has dropped to about eight percent.

There are times when non-profit landlords have to borrow to finance some of their new construction activities. This does not mean that they are completely dependent on the capital market, though. Social landlords are still able to arrange heavily subsidized loans, but only in Germany. Nonetheless, loans can also be arranged under those conditions on the capital market. In that event, a supplementary interest subsidy is provided. In 1994, roughly 49 percent of the financing needed in Germany nationwide came directly from the capital market. The fact that this proportion is increasing is not seen as a problem. The reason is that the government subsidizes and guarantees a great deal of this capital financing.

In some countries, it is not the government but an umbrella organization that actively solicits the loans and subsequently makes them available to individual landlords. This is the route taken in Belgium by the regional housing societies. They take care of the financing for social rented dwellings built by authorized building contractors. In France, it is the Caisse des Dépôts et Consignations (CDC) that solicits the financing for the HLM institutions. In England, Sweden, Denmark, and the Netherlands, however, there is no alternative to the capital market. The financing in Sweden and Denmark is primarily provided by mortgage banks. In Denmark, the financing procedure has to take place according to strictly defined rules. This legislation stipulates which institutions are allowed to extend long-term loans on real estate. It covers the way in which the capital for these loans is supposed to be obtained. The law specifies the conditions under which these loans may be offered and sets the guarantee requirements. In practice, only three financial institutions are involved in housing finance. Like the German social landlords, the Dutch and English landlords also borrow directly from the capital market. In addi-

Table 9.2 Source of the financial means needed for investment in the non-profit rented sector (new construction) in the seven West European countries, 1994-1995 (percentages)

	Own assets	Borrowing	Lump-sum subsidies
Netherlands	9	83	8
Belgium	20	59	21
England	-	58	42
Denmark	2	91	7
Germany	33	49	18
France	3	80	17
Sweden	3	95	2

Source: OTB survey on financing in the social rented sector, 1996.

tion to the Bank Dutch Municipalities Ltd, it is often pension funds and insurance companies that provide the financing in the Netherlands, though they often do so through an intermediary or another organization. The Dutch situation is unique in another sense. Some of the richer housing associations have started to provide financing for their own sector. Banks and building societies (mortgage banks) also play a major role in housing finance in England too. Recent studies on the attitude of the financial institutions toward lending to housing associations identify the two main reasons why banks and building societies have turned to financing the social sector. These are the relatively favorable position of the associations, and the good relationship between profit and risk.

9.6 The risk and guarantee structure

The fifth research question deals with the risk and guarantee structure in the social rented sector in the seven countries under study. The sixth question concerns the conditions that are posed by the financiers. Of course, the risk structure is strongly linked to the institution that ultimately solicits the loans. In Belgium and France, as mentioned earlier, intermediary organizations are responsible for the loans that are solicited on the capital market and subsequently passed on to the social landlords. If a French HLM institution wants to take out a subsidized loan, the organization is obligated to subscribe to a guarantee system. This system is set up as an insurance scheme. It kicks in when an HLM is unable to meet its financial obligations. The guarantee institution for the social rented sector is managed by the CDC and is under the supervision of an administrative board. In Belgium, the intermediary housing societies are covered by the regional governments.

In countries where the social landlords have to turn directly to the capital market, the risks are different, of course. In the Netherlands, an extensive guarantee system has been developed in order to limit the risk. The Guarantee Fund for Social Housing Construction (WSW) plays a crucial role in that system. Housing associations that borrow with a guarantee by the WSW can count on a three-pronged security package. The primary security is formed by the financial resilience of the housing association itself and the backup provided by the Central Housing Fund. The secondary security consists of the assets of the WSW. Those assets are formed by a lump-sum deposit by the state and the contributions that associations make to the WSW in exchange for the guarantee. The tertiary security is formed by the state and the municipalities, which provide backup support on a fifty-fifty basis. Lenders have great confidence in the fund, which is reflected in the favorable interest rates on the loans that carry a WSW guarantee. In Denmark, the state and the municipality jointly guarantee the building loans that non-profit institutions solicit from specific mortgage banks. To finance dwelling improvement, the umbrella organization of non-profit landlords provides a guarantee for the share of the financing that is not guaranteed by the municipality.

In Germany and Sweden too, the government plays a key role in guaranteeing loans for social housing construction. Virtually all the risks are covered in this manner. In Sweden, the landlords do have to pay a premium for the state guarantee. Without this risk insurance, it is impossible for non-profit landlords to get 100 percent financing on the capital market.

Unlike the above countries, the loans of the English housing associations are not guaranteed in a formal sense. Nevertheless, the regulation of the Housing Corporation and the political support ensure that the loans to housing associations have a low risk profile. In this way, assets can be accumulated that financiers will consider acceptable as collateral for the loans. In addition, the public subsidies are secondary to the private financing. In other words, if it is necessary to draw upon the collateral, the private lender will be reimbursed first, before the housing corporation gets back any portion of the subsidy. The attraction for private financiers lies in a solid, risk-reducing government subsidy, a steady cash flow, and a good reputation. That reputation is guarded by the Housing Corporation, in its supplementary role as controller of those in which it invests.

In sum, it appears that in most of the countries studied, similar guarantees are provided for loans that are arranged by social landlords on the capital market, either directly or indirectly. England forms the exception. Furthermore, it appears that the risk to lenders are very limited.

9.7 The volume of demand for financing

The annual demand for financing in the seven countries studied here is determined by the volume of new construction, the average construction cost, and the share of the total financing that is derived from external sources. That external financing is the amount that does not come out of own assets or from lump-sum subsidies. Table 9.3 shows this information for the seven countries considered here. It should be kept in mind that this table refers to an estimate of the total financing demand for new construction projects in the social rented sector. Furthermore, it should be noted that the annual fluctuations can be great. The financing of other activities such as urban renewal, acquisition, and dwelling improvement are not taken into consideration. In many countries, these other activities constitute an important part of the range of tasks carried out by social landlords.

As Table 9.3 indicates, the total demand for financing in Germany is by far the greatest, at NLG 36.5 billion. This demand is created by fact that, relative to other countries, the construction costs in Germany are extremely high, running NLG 460,000 per dwelling on average. The high volume of demand is also caused by the extensive program of new construction, producing 162,000 dwellings per year. The demand for financing in the other six countries is negligible in comparison. For example, in France, the country that is next on the list, has a demand of roughly NLG 5.2 billion per year. Belgium and Denmark trail the rest, with 257 and 609 million guilders, respectively.

Table 9.3 Estimated new construction (x 1,000 dwellings), average construction cost per unit (x NLG 1,000), percentage of external financing, and total demand for external financing (x NLG 1,000) in the non-profit rented sector (new construction) in seven West European countries in 1995

	New construction	Average construction cost	External financing	Total demand for external financing
Netherland	23.8	140	83	2,766,000
Belgium	3.3	151	59	257,000
England	31.6	116	58	2,126,000
Denmark	3	219	91	609,000
Germany	162	460	49	36,515,000
France	62	133	79	5,240,000
Sweden	4.9	225	95	1,068,000

Source: OTB survey on financing in the social rented sector, 1996.

9.8 Interest rates and the providers of capital

The eighth and ninth research questions revolve around interest rates, types of lenders, and the market share of these lenders. In most countries, financing in the social rented sector is provided by institutional investors and banks. In the Netherlands, banks have recently joined the group of lenders of this sector. Besides investors and banks, municipalities are also active (to a limited extent) in providing loans to housing associations. Another way in which the Netherlands is unique is in the emergence of collegiality in arranging financing. This means that rich housing associations extend low-cost loans to their poorer colleague associations that have a building program to complete. The financing of the German and French social rented dwellings is also provided by a wide range of financiers. These include credit institutions, savings banks, private and social insurance companies, building savings banks, and other lenders. In France, the subsidized loans are arranged by a specific intermediary organization (CDC). In Belgium, the long-term public loans to the regional housing societies are provided not only by institutional investors; they are also extended by private parties. In Denmark and Sweden, the financing institutions have special stock issues that are traded on the stock exchange.

In order to gain deeper insight in the characteristics of the loans that have been extended, Table 9.4 highlights the type of loan, the average interest rate, and the difference in interest on loans solicited by non-profit landlords and those solicited by the state. Of course, municipalities can also take out loans on the capital market. Therefore, the table also shows the differential in interest rates between the loans taken out by the state and those taken out by the municipalities on the capital market. The risk is limited in all the countries studied and, in many cases, the loans are guaranteed. Under these conditions, the social landlords are able to arrange financing on the capital market at fairly reasonable rates. In most cases, the interest

Table 9.4   Type of loan, nominal interest rate, the differential between loans contracted by non-profit landlords and government loans and the differential between the interest rates on loans contracted by the state and the municipalities, in seven West European countries in 1995

	Type of loan	Interest rate (%)	Differential with respect to government loans (%)	Differential Governm. loans to municipal loans (%)
Netherlands	annuity (70%)/fixe	7.5	0.25	0.15
Belgium	annuity	7.1	0.14	not applicable
England[1)]	annuity/linear	8.0	1.3	0.8[2)]
Denmark	index	3.6	not applicable	not applicable
Germany[1)]	annuity	7.0	1.5	0.15
France	annuity	5.8	2.0	0.5
Sweden	annuity(80%)/linear	10.7	1.73	0.5

[1)] 1994
[2)] Estimate
Source: OTB survey on financing in the social rented sector, 1996.

differential --that is, the differential between the contracted interest rate and that charged on government loans-- is merely a few tenths of a percent higher than the interest on loans that are contracted by the state. It is not easy to give an unambiguous explanation for the differences between the countries studied here. The reason is that the interest differential is determined by two situations. First of all, the degree to which the risks are assessed by the lenders plays a significant role. Secondly, the efficiency, competition, and ordering of the money market in the various countries exert an influence. If only a few lenders are active in a country, the chance of relatively expensive loans increases sharply. When the competition between diverse lenders is stiff, however, the interest rates will generally be calculated with the consumer in mind. A similar situation exists in the Netherlands, for instance. In nearly all of the countries studied, this external financing is arranged by way of annuity loans.

The exception to this pattern is Denmark. There, indexed loans are required. Sweden and England still have the linear loan alongside the annuity loan, although the linear loan is becoming scarce. The fixed loan is specific to the Netherlands. With a fixed loan, only the interest has to be paid in the course of the loan. After the contract expires, the principal is paid off in its entirety.

9.9 Financing opportunities for foreign lenders

The opportunities for interested foreign lenders to invest in the social rented sector in one of the seven countries studied here differ widely. The best opportunities seem to be found in England. In practice, this market has already been penetrated by various foreign banks. In light of the persistently high demand for private financing, the opportunities for participation in this market will probably be ample in the near future as well. The biggest potential market is not found in England, however, but in Germany. Despite this enormous potential --the financing of construction in the social housing sector involves the tidy sum of NLG 36 billion-- the opportunities for foreign lenders in Germany are meager compared to those in England. In this respect, various reports demonstrate that there is no lack of opportunities for potential lenders in German social housing. Furthermore, on the basis of the current system of subsidization and financing, it would seem improbable that foreign lenders would be able to get a foot in the door in the German social housing construction sector. Only in the event that the present system would be changed and stabilized is it likely that new opportunities would arise. It is particularly the opportunities to make a profit on the operation of social rented dwellings that is an interesting area in Germany.

There are also opportunities for foreign lenders in the Netherlands. The market for loans to housing associations in the Netherlands is completely open to foreign financial institutions. The need for investment in the housing associations will remain fairly sizable in the coming years (five to 6 billion guilders per year). Because of the guarantee structure of the WSW and the CFV, loans to housing associations in the Netherlands are a safe investment. Loans to Dutch housing associations might possibly serve to diversify the portfolio of foreign investors. Loans from foreign financiers might be a good alternative for loans from the Dutch government.

French and Belgian social landlords arrange for loans through special financing institutions. Therefore, there are only limited opportunities available for external financiers to extend loans to individual institutions. What is possible in these countries is to extend a loan directly to the intermediary financial organizations. In this regard, in France, the Caisse des Dépôts et Consignations (CDC) is an option. The CDC has a monopoly in the financing of social rented dwellings. The CDC derives its capital from savings banks, pension funds, and other financial institutions. The extension of loans to the French HLM institutions to be used for other activities is not entirely free of risk. Relatively many HLM institutions have run into cash-flow problems in recent years. It is clear that such problems involve risks. This is also demonstrated by the fact that the differential between the interest on government loans and the interest on the loans made to HLM institutions was estimated to be about two percent by informants who responded to our questionnaire.

The limited range of opportunities in Belgium is caused first of all by the very low level of production of social rented dwellings. At approximately 3,000 completions per year, this production is among the lowest in Western Europe. Furthermore, almost half of the required funds are covered by the building contractors' own assets and the government subsidies. Moreover, just about the only entities that can contract loans are the three regional housing societies. The risk that lenders run in lending to those societies is extremely low. The reason is that those societies are financially covered by regional governments. The slight risk also means that the interest rates are exceptionally low. They only exceed the level for regional government loans by about 0.14 percent.

In Denmark too, it is impossible to ignore the financial institutions that are mentioned by name in the law. It is possible, however, to acquire special bonds or specifically mortgage bonds from the three authorized mortgage institutions. In practice, the investors in Denmark equate these bonds with government bonds. In the event of the mortgage institution going bankrupt, the holders of mortgage bonds would have priority over other creditors. Indirectly, there are thus definitely good opportunities for investors and banks to invest in the Danish non-profit rented sector. The interest that is repaid on the bonds is limited, however. This is caused in part by the fact that institutional investors do not have to pay taxes on income from bonds based on indexed loans. For that reason, the interest level of the indexed bonds is lower than the interest on nominal bonds. The slight risk that they entail is the reason why the difference between the interest that the lender has to pay and the interest that the mortgage institution reimburses to the holder of the mortgage bond is a mere 0.3 to 0.5 percent.

Finally, in Sweden, the low solvency of the non-profit rented sector does not have to prevent external lenders from offering loans to the non-profit institutions. The municipal housing companies are in fact public organizations that are fully covered financially by the local authorities. Therefore, the risk that external lenders would have to carry is very low. In this case, a high solvency is not actually necessary. The financing runs directly through the capital market, and only mortgage banks act as intermediary agencies. Therefore, the institutional structure does not pose any obstacles either. In addition, the possible yield is reasonably high

Summarizing, it can be posed that of the seven countries studied here, England offers the best opportunities for foreign lenders to invest in the social rented sector. In the Netherlands too, there are certainly good opportunities. Despite the potential opportunities in Germany, fewer actual opportunities are available there for the time being. First of all, Germany's financing system needs to be stabilized. The French and Belgian social landlords draw their loans from special financing institutions. Therefore, these two countries have only limited opportunities to extend loans directly to individual landlords. And the highly regulated Danish financial market offers few opportunities for foreign investors. The institutional structure in Sweden does not pose any obstacles. In addition, the possible yield is reasonably high.

REFERENCES

Aughton, H. and P. Malpass, 1994, **Housing Finance,** Fourth Edition, Shelter, London.

Ball, M., 1994, European financial liberalisation and property markets, in: W. Bartlett and G. Bramley (eds.), **European housing finance, single market or mosaic?**, SAUS, Bristol.

Bartlett, W. and G. Bramley, 1994, **European housing finance, single market or mosaic?**, SAUS, Bristol.

Batselier, N. de, 1994, **Leefbaar wonen in Vlaanderen**. Beleidsnota Huisvesting, Vlaams ministerie van Huisvesting, Brussel.

Bengtsson, P., 1994, The housing market and housing finance in Sweden, in: Bartlett, W. e.a. (eds.), **European Housing Finance**, Bristol (SAUS) pp.187-198.

BLR, 1996, **Questionnaire response: private finance for social housing,** Berlin.

Boelhouwer, P.J., en H.M.H. van der Heijden, 1992, **Vergelijkende studie naar volkshuisvestingssystemen in Europa. Algemeen beleidskader**, Zoetermeer (DGVH).

Boléat, M., 1987, **International housing finance factbook 1987,** London (IUBS-SA).

Boléat, M., 1989, **Housing in Britain**, Londen (The Building Societies Association).

Boligministeriet (Danish Ministry of Housing and Building), 1984, **Financing of Housing in Denmark**, Copenhagen.

Boligministeriet (Danish Ministry of Housing and Building), 1988a, **Non-profit housing in Denmark**, Copenhagen.

Boligministeriet (Danish Ministry of Housing and Building), 1994, **The role of private rental housing in the housing market**, Copenhagen.

Boligstyrelsen, 1989, **Beretning fra tilsynet med realkreditinstitutter**, Kopenhagen.

Boucher, F., 1988, France, in: Kroes, H., F. Ymkers en A. Mulder (eds.) **Between owner-occupation and rented sector**, De Bilt (NCIV), pp.145-182.

Bouwmans, R.N.J., 1995, Tussen sociale doelstelling en financiële continuïteit, **Corporatie Magazine,** nr. 14, pp.6-10.

Bouwmans, R.N.J., 1996, Betaalbaarheid blijft knelpunt onder nieuw IHS-stelsel, **Corporatie Magazine,** nr. 3, pp.4-7.

Bramley, G., 1993, The enabling role for local authorities: a preliminary evaluation, in: Malpass, P. en R. Means (eds.) **Implementing Housing Policy**, Open University Press, Buckingham, pp.127-149.

Bundesministerium, 1992, **Wohngeld und Mietbericht,** 1991, Bundesministerium für Raumordnung, Bauwesen und Städtebau, Bonn.

Bundesministerium, 1993, **Haus und Wohnung: Im Spiegel der Statistik 1993,** Bundesministerium für Raumordnung, Bauwesen und Städtebau, Bonn.

CBS, 1996, **Maandstatistiek bouwnijverheid,** maart 1996, Voorburg/Heerlen (Centraal Bureau voor de Statistiek).

CECODHAS, 1994, **Social housing in the European Union, which public policies up to the year 2000**, L'observatoire Européen du Logement Social, special issue, May 1994, Paris.

CFV, 1996, **Jaarverslag 1995,** Huizen (Centraal Fonds voor de Volkshuisvesting).

COFACE, 1989, **Social housing policy, Federal republic of Germany, Housing Commission Report,** COFACE, Brussels.

Collignon, R., N. de Batselier en D. Gosuin, 1993, **Financiering van de sociale Huisvesting**, vijfde vergadering van de Europese ministers bevoegd voor huisvesting, EG, Brussel.

Cruyce, A. van den en K. van Dender, 1993, **Financiering van de sociale woningbouw in Vlaanderen**, Leuven (Hoger Instituut voor de Arbeid).

Dieten, J. van, 1996, Interview met prof. ir. W. Keeris, **Corporatie Magazine**, nr. 3, pp.12-15.

DIW, 1996, **Questionnaire response: private finance for social housing,** Berlin.

Dolder, B. van den, 1994, De oude en nieuwe waarborgen van het WSW, **Corporatiemagazine,** nr. 14, pp.4-6.

Eekhoff, J., 1989, Wohnungspolitik für die neunziger Jahre: Muss der staat wieder Verstärkt eingreifen? **Gemeinnütziges Wohnungswesen,** 7/1989, 371-378.

Emms, P., 1990, **Social Housing, A European dilemma?**, School for Advanced Urban Studies, Bristol.

Englund, P., 1993, **The Collapse of the Swedish Housing Market**, Uppsala, Sweden.

European Commission, 1993, **Statistics on Housing in the European Community**, E.C. Brussels.

European Commission, 1994, **Statistics on Housing in the European Community**, E.C. Brussels.

Fribourg, A.M., 1994, **Mimeograpf**, Ministère du Logement, Parijs.

GdW, 1992, **GdW Bericht 1991/92,** GdW, Köln.

GdW, 1993, **GdW Bericht 1992/93,** GdW, Köln.

Gerrichhauzen, L.G., en M. van Giessen, 1984, België: een geprivatiseerd en gedereguleerd woonparadijs?, **Volkshuisvesting, 36**, nr. 7, pp.305-313.

Ghékiere, L., 1993, **Patrimoines locatifs sociaux: politiques de vente comparées des Etats de la CEE**, in Maastricht: Enjeux por le mouvement HLM, Report from 54th HLM Congress, June 1993, UNFOHLM, Paris, pp.31-37.

Gibb, K. and M. Munro, 1991, **Housing Finance in the UK: An Introduction,** Macmillan, London.

Goossens, L., 1993, Volkshuisvestingsbeleid in België (Vlaanderen), in: Rietman en Derksen (red.), Volkshuisvesting vergeleken, pp.57-74.

Gruis, V., 1996, **Waardering tegen bedrijfswaarde door woningcorporaties,** Delft (afstudeerverslag).

Haffner, M.E.A., 1992, **Eigen woning in de EG: fiscale en overige financiële instrumenten.** Delft (DUP).

Hägred, U., 1993, **The changing role of the nonprofit housing sector in Sweden**, Swedish Board of Housing, Building and Planning, Karlskrona.

Harten, J.G. van, 1990, Sociale verhuurders in problemen door hoogbouw, **Woningraad-Magazine,** nr. 15, pp.39-42.

Harten, J.G. van, en H.B.H.G. Wilke, 1993, Huuronderhandelingen in Zweden: Mag het iets minder zijn? in: **Woningraad-Magazine**, nr. 5, pp.7-11.

Hallet, G., 1993, **The new Housing Shortage: Housing Affordability in Europe and the USA,** Routledge, London.

Hayes, S., 1996, Finance: Better terms, **Housing**, April, p.22.

Heerma, E., 1993, **Besluit woninggebonden subsidies per 1995,** brief aan de Tweede Kamer, 21 september.

Hees, C. van, 1996, Waarborgfonds Sociale Woningbouw viert koperen jubileum; 'Moetje' groeit uit tot voorbeeldige publiek-private samenwerking, **Woningraad-Magazine,** nr. 11, pp.36-38.

Heugas-Darraspen, H., 1985, **Le logement en France et son financement**, Paris (La Documentation Française).

Hills, J., F. Hubert, H. Tomann and C. Whitehead, 1990, Shifting Subsidies from Bricks and Mortar to People: Experiences in Britain and West-Germany, **Housing Studies,** 5 (3), pp.147-167

Housing Associations Weekly, 1996a, 'Right to buy could mean sale of 2,000 homes, HA's tell Corporation, **HA Weekly,** 12th January, p.1.

Housing Associations Weekly, 1996b, Marriage of convenience, **HA Weekly,** 15th March, p.13.

Housing Corporation, 1994, **1994/5 Annual Report**, Housing Corporation, London.

Housing Corporation, 1995, **Private Finance Survey**, Housing Corporation, London.

Housing Corporation, 1996a, **1996/97 ADP Bulletin**, March 1996, Housing Corporation, London.

Housing Corporation, 1996b, **Private Finance Forecast**, April 1996, Number 5, Housing Corporation, London.

Hubert, F., 1992, **Risk and Incentives in German Social Housing Finance,** Free University of Berlin, Berlin.

Joseph Rowntree Foundation, 1996, The outlook for Housing Investment Trusts, **Housing Summary 14,** JRF, York.

Kellersmann, G., 1996, Maatschappelijk rendement als zesde verantwoordingsveld, **Corporatie Magazine**, nr. 11, p.4-9.

Kemp, P., 1993, Rebuilding the private rented sector?, in: Malpass, P. and R. Means (eds.), **Implementing Housing Policy**, Open University Press, Buckingham.

Klieverik, H., 1996, De huur wordt straks in euro's betaald, **Woningraad**, nr. 21, pp.8-9.

Koopman, J.M., 1992, Het Zweedse model: selectief gebruiken graag, **Corporatie-magazine**, nr. 20, pp.28-32.

Lindencrona, T., 1994, **Municipal Housing Companies in Sweden**, Stockholm (SABO).

Lopategui, T., 1996, Lending for a longer run, **Chartered Banker**, January, p.13.

Marchal, J., 1989, **Social housing policy, France**, Brussels (C.O.F.A.C.E housing commission documents).

McCrone, G. and Stephens, M., 1995, **Housing Policy in Britain and Europe,** UCL Press, London.

Menkveld, A.J., 1992, **Internationale vergelijking van de woonuitgaven, een macro-analyse**, Delft (DUP).

Menkveld, A.J., 1993, **Internationale vergelijking van de woonuitgaven, een micro-analyse**, Delft (DUP).

Mew, B., 1995, The state of the LSVT market, **Voluntary Housing**, February, pp.26-29.

Middelaar, G.W. van, 1995, Brutering en jaarrekening: ontwerp-richtlijn aangevuld, **Corporatiemagazine,** nr. 7, pp.30-32.

MVROM, 1989, **Nota Volkshuisvesting in de Jaren Negentig; van bouwen naar wonen**, 's-Gravenhage, Tweede Kamer, 20.691, nrs. 2-3.

Ministerie van VROM, 1992, **MG 92-38**.

Ministry of Housing and Building, 1984, **Financing of housing in Denmark**, Kopenhagen.

NEI, 1989, **Volkshuisvestingsbeleid in Europa, fase 1**, Beknopt overzicht van het beleid in een aantal geselecteerde landen, Rotterdam (NEI).

NCIV, 1995, Aangepaste berekening financieringsruimte bij het WSW, **Werkwijzer**, nr. 120.

NCIV, 1996, Sector moet 20 miljard onrendabel investeren, **Corporatiemagazine**, nr. 9, pp.19.

NFHA, 1995, **Competence and accountability: The report of the inquiry into housing association governance**, National Federation of Housing Associations, London.

NMH, 1988, Jaarverslag 1987, Brussel.

Noordenne, M. van, 1996, Leefbaarheid en de rol van woningcorporaties, **Corporatie Magazine**, nr. 7, p.6-9.

Norton, A. and Novy, K., 1991, **Low Income Housing in Britain and Germany**, Anglo-German Foundation for the Study of Industrial Society, London.

NWR, 1993, Verzelfstandiging geregeld; BBSH in de praktijk, **Woningraad Extra**, nr. 63.

Omme, A.M. van, 1992, **Besluit beheer sociale-huursector: prestaties en verantwoording**, 's-Gravenhage (VNG-uitgeverij).

Oxley, M.J., 1995, Private and Social Rented Housing in Europe: Distinctions, Comparisons and Resource Allocation, **Scandinavian Journal of Housing and Planning Research,** Vol. 12, No. 2.

Oxley, M.J. and Smith, J.E., 1996, **Housing Policy and Rented Housing in Europe,** E&FN Spon, London.

Papa, O.A., 1992, **Een vergelijkende Europese studie naar volkshuisvestingssystemen, Financiële instrumenten in het volkshuisvestingsbeleid,** Zoetermeer (VROM/DGVH).

Pearse, B., 1996, Helping to build the homes of the future, **Chartered Banker**, January, p.13.

Perry, J., 1996, Long live the revolution, **Inside Housing**, 19th April, pp.14-15.

Power, A., 1993, **Hovels to High Rise: State Housing in Europe since 1850**, Routledge, London.

Priemus, H., 1995, How to abolish social housing? The Dutch case, **International Journal of Urban and Regional Research**, volume 19, nr. 1.

Priemus, H., verschijnt binnenkort, Recent Changes in the Social Rented Sector in The Netherlands, in: **Urban Studies; An International Journal for Research in Urban and Regional Studie**s.

Pryke, M. and C. Whitehead, 1991, An overview of recent change in the provision of private finance for social housing, **Discussion Paper 18**, Department of Land Economy, University of Cambridge.

Pryke, M. and C. Whitehead, 1995, Private finance and the risks of social housing provision, **Discussion Paper 46**, Department of Land Economy, University of Cambridge.

Randall, S., 1996, Dreaming of a big HIT, **Inside Housing**, 10th May, pp.12-13.

Realkreditradet, 1990, **Annual report 1989**, Copenhagen.

Reyger, A. de, 1996, Kanttekeningen bij het prognosemodel sociale-huursector, **Nieuw tijdschrift voor de volkshuisvesting**, nr.5, p.11-13.

Rietman, H.C.I., 1993, **Volkshuisvesting in Nederland en België**, Zwolle, (Tjeenk Willink) (proefschrift).

SABO, 1993, **Municipal Housing Companies Experiences in Sweden**, Stockholm (SABO).

SCB, 1992, Bostads- och byggnadsstatistisk Arsbok 1992, Stockholm.

Schaar, J. van der, 1991, **Volkshuisvesting: een zaak van beleid**, Utrecht (Het Spectrum).

Scheers, J., 1986, **De huisvestingsmarkt: Dit is België. Analyse, model en dynamieken toegepast op de agglomeratie Brussel**, KU-Leuven, departement sociologie.

SEV, 1992, **De huursombenadering; de experimenten nader beschouwd,** Rotterdam (Stichting Experimenten Volkshuisvesting).

SEO, 1993, **Het noodzakelijke weerstandsvermogen van corporaties,** Amsterdam (SEO).

Skifter Andersen, H., 1994, **The role of non-profit housing in housing policy in Northern Europe - the case of Denmark,** Copenhagen (Danish Building Research Institute).

Spijkers, P.A.W.M., 1994, Financiering van de woningbouw; nieuwe spelregels voor corporaties, **Bouw,** nr. 16/17, pp.10-11.

Statistisches Bundesamt, 1990, Bewilligungen in sozialen Wohnungsbau, **Bautätigkeit,** Fachserie 5, Reihe 2, Wiesbaden.

Statistisches Bundesamt, 1991, Bewilligungen in sozialen Wohnungsbau, **Bautätigkeit,** Fachserie 5, Reihe 2, Wiesbaden.

Statistisches Bundesamt, 1994, Bewilligungen in sozialen Wohnungsbau, **Bautätigkeit,** Fachserie 5, Reihe 2, Wiesbaden.

Tomann, H., 1990, Housing in West Germany, in: Maclennan, D. and R. Williams (eds.), **Affordable Housing in Europe,** Joseph Rowntree Foundation, York.

Tomann, H., 1994, Government intervention and regulation: Effects on housing finance, **Housing Finance International,** June, pp 16-21.

Tommel, D.K.J., 1996, **Prognosemodel sociale-huursector,** brief aan de Tweede Kamer DBD 22896031, Den Haag, MVROM.

UNFOHLM, 1994, Germany: Draft reform of subsidy to social housing, News Bulletin no. 1, January 1994, Observatory on European Social Housing, Paris.

Ven, B.L.M. van de, 1995, **Vergelijkende studie naar volkshuisvestingssystemen in Europa,** Delft (DUP).

Venema, S., 1994, Van een rode ceintuur naar een zwarte band, **De Volkskrant,** 28 mei.

Voluntary Housing, 1995, LSVTs: A part of the movement, **Voluntary Housing,** February, p.25.

Wells, A., 1996, City Money, **Housing,** April, pp.26-27.

Westergard, K., 1989, **Social housing policy Denmark**, COFACE housing commission documents, EG, Brussel.

Wilcox, S., 1995, **Housing Finance Review 1995/96**, Joseph Rowntree Foundation, York.

Wilcox, S. and J. Hawksworth, 1995, Living on borrowed time, **Roof**, July/August, p.11.

Wiktorin, M., 1992, **An international comparison of rent setting and conflict resolution**, Input report for an evaluation of the Swedish system of utility-value rent setting, Swedish Institute for Building Research, Gävle, Sweden.

WSW, 1994, **Dokumentatieset November 1994,** Huizen (Waarborgfonds Sociale Woningbouw).

VERSCHENEN IN DE SERIE HOUSING AND URBAN POLICY STUDIES

1. Peter Boelhouwer en Harry van der Heijden, Housing systems in Europe: Part I, a comparative study of housing policy
 1992/298 blz./ISBN 90-6275-769-3/ƒ 63,60
2. Oscar Papa, Housing systems in Europe: Part II, a comparative study of housing finance
 1992/210 blz./ISBN 90-6275-770-7/ƒ 49,80
3. Lennart J. Lundqvist, Dislodging the welfare state? Housing and privatization in four European nations
 1992/144 blz./ISBN 90-6275-771-5/ƒ 45,-
4. Henk Gilhuis en Sjoukje Volbeda, Collective self-help housing in Brazil
 1992/176 blz./ISBN 90-6275-672-7/ƒ 49,80
5. Hugo Priemus and Gerard Metselaar, Urban renewal policy in a European perspective, an international comparative analysis
 1992/68 blz./ISBN 90-6275-787-1/ƒ 23,85
6. Hugo Priemus, Mark Kleinmann, Duncan Maclennan and Bengt Turner, European monetary, economic and political union: consequences for national housing policies
 1993/57 blz./ISBN 90-6275-840-1/ƒ 17,50
7. Henk Visscher, Building control in five European countries
 1993/162 blz./ISBN 90-6275-908-4/ƒ 43,-
8. Helen Kruythoff, Residential environments and households in the Randstad
 1993/241 blz./ISBN 90-6275-927-0/ƒ 63,60
9. Berth Danermark and Ingemar Elander, Social rented housing in Europe: policy, tenure and design
 1994/182 blz./ISBN 90-6275-942-4/ƒ 45,-
10. Godfrey Anyumba, Kisumu Town: history of the built form, planning and environment: 1890-1990
 1995/372 blz./ISBN 90-407-1067-8/ƒ 95,40
11. P.J. Boelhouwer en A.J. Menkveld, Housing expenditure in Western Europe: macro and micro quotas
 1996/58 blz./ISBN 90-407-1327-8/ƒ 17,50

12. J.E. Smith, What determines housing investment? An investigation into the social, economic and political determinants of housing investment in four European countries
Verschijnt binnenkort